HAUNTED
SHEFFIELD

HAUNTED
SHEFFIELD

MR AND MRS P. DREADFUL

TEMPUS

First published 2006

Tempus Publishing Limited
The Mill, Brimscombe Port,
Stroud, Gloucestershire, GL5 2QG
www.tempus-publishing.com

British Library Cataloguing in Publication Data.
A catalogue record for this book is available from the British Library.

ISBN 978 0 7524 4195 7

Typesetting and origination by Tempus Publishing Limited.
Printed in Great Britain.

CONTENTS

Acknowledgements   6

Introduction   7

1   The Central City and Town Hall   9

2   Campo Lane and the Old City   39

3   Exchange Street to Ponds Forge   63

4   The Don and Around   77

Bibliography   95

ACKNOWLEDGEMENTS

The modern photographs used in the book were taken by Steve Harrison and all the old images were supplied courtesy of Sheffield City Libraries.

INTRODUCTION

Sheffield is the fifth largest city in England and has been a place of human habitation since at least the twelfth century; the forest and moorland that surrounded the small settlement were cut down and turned to the farmer's plough and roaming sheep. The first markets here were recorded in 1296 as well as the mill that ground the wheat, corn and barley that was grown here. The age of 'Sheaf field' is something that most visitors miss, thinking that the city grew up in the Georgian period (1714-1830), but the city itself was laid out along the River Don well before that; its fame for steelmaking is even referred to in Chaucer's *Canterbury Tales*.

Many of the ghostly stories contained in this book are eye-witness accounts and personal stories of ordinary folk from Sheffield who work, play and raise families in the city. Some ghosts share their old homes or workplaces with modern people who now live or work there. Some make a nuisance of themselves and others are harmless, even funny. Some of the ghost stories included here, and the background to them, have come to me through research at the tables of the Sheffield Central Library where the staff have been so helpful, even though I often seemed to be asking for original material that was missing, sometimes due apparently to Hitler's remodelling of the city years ago!

There are always plenty of tales to tell but research and confirmation of the stories comes first and there are plenty of tales that have been left out of this collection because the stories couldn't be substantiated or didn't stand up to scrutiny.

Sheffield's history is old, older than many of us perhaps are aware, and wherever there is life, there is death. Some of the Sheffield dead don't sleep deeply and come back to visit their relatives or to have a look at the city they once knew. So if you find yourself walking through the quiet streets of Sheffield of an evening, remember you may not be alone: the ghosts of the past are always with you. Just because you can't see them doesn't mean they are not there. They might try to reach out to you, as many others have found to their great surprise!

Yours truly,
Mr P. Dreadful.

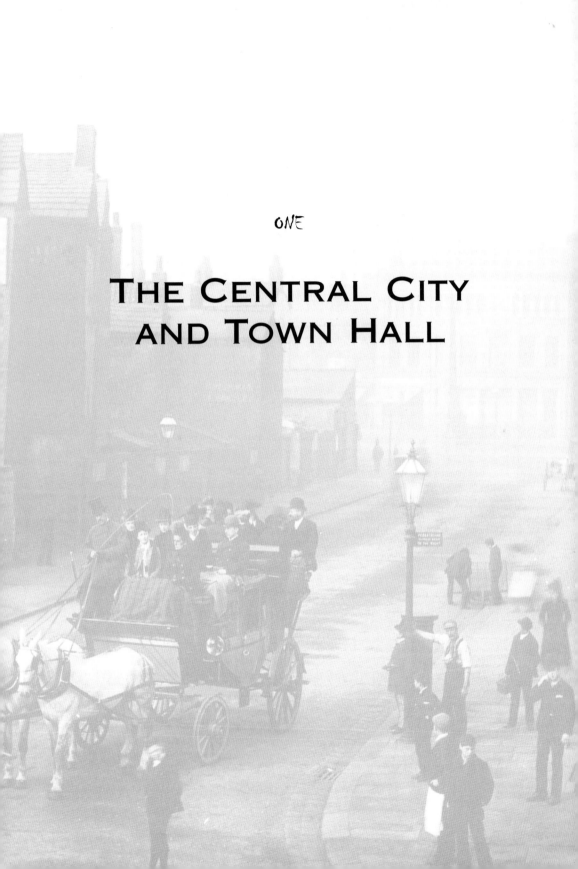

ONE

THE CENTRAL CITY
AND TOWN HALL

THE CENTRAL CITY AND TOWN HALL

The Wicker Herbal (Norfolk Street)

This story starts in the old grounds of the Sheffield Medical School that was on the grounds of the current Central Library (built in 1926). The ghost that inhabits The Wicker Herbal was said to be a poor unfortunate who was taken to the morgue there, but was not entirely dead. The Medical School had a hard time finding bodies to supply the dissection tables and this poor soul who still inhabits The Wicker Herbal was one of those unfortunates who was pressed into the search for truth and scientific advancement.

Now you're wondering how the ghost could travel from one building to another? Well, when the medical school closed, the entire fittings were sold off and some went to a nearby business, Hibbert Brothers, purveyors of artist's materials to the people of Sheffield. They mixed their own paints using linseed and expensive pigments for their Victorian clients, so when the medical school closed they bought four marble slabs that had been used for dissection and autopsy. Hibbert Brothers closed in the late 1990s and The Wicker Herbal took over the premises with its deep cold cellars and the marble tables. For some reason the ghost became active during the refitting of the shop, which was undertaken to convert the premises into the herbal shop it is today.

The ghost itself made its presence felt by dropping packets and pills from the high shelves onto the client's heads. The strange fact about this is that the treatments it drops from above are usually the very things the person has come in to look for, as if the ghost has made a diagnosis for the person it picks on and then tries to help him or her. The ghost also has another trick up its sleeve; it puts packets and bottles into the open pockets or purses of unwitting customers and on more than one occasion the staff have had to run after an unintentional shoplifter who is mortified to find he or she is carrying something from the top shelf of which he had no knowledge.

There used to be a vegan restaurant on the same premises, above the shop, called the Olive Garden, and this tale is one of my own experience when visiting the Wicker Herbal once with my wife. We were sitting at a table in the quiet restaurant eating lunch when the cutlery on a nearby table began to vibrate and shift across the surface of the cotton cloth. The floor of the restaurant was bare wood and solid, the tables themselves were metal and thin legged so the vibration from the road outside would have had trouble coming up through the legs and onto the wooden surface of the table and through the heavy cotton tablecloth. My wife checked

The art shop in Surrey Street that became the Wicker Herbal. The ghost here tries to help the shop's customers.

outside for any heavy traffic that might have been passing or for any other activity in the restaurant that might offer an explanation. We were alone apart from a waiter who was polishing cutlery behind a small wall. We considered that perhaps a ghost was trying to pick up a fork and knife hoping to join us for dinner. The knife and fork travelled across the surface toward our table and eventually fell to the floor while we ate in silence, watching the progress of the cutlery. After we'd finished we asked the waiter on duty if he'd seen cutlery fall off the tables before. We didn't get a direct answer but he did smile and asked us if we enjoyed our lunch! The look on his face was one of quiet sufferance – perhaps that was the reason he spent so much time repolishing the cutlery! This was not the only 'encounter' we had with a ghost at The Wicker Herbal. The next activity involved a modern contrivance, a computer.

The Wicker Herbal downstairs had a touch screen computer that allowed the customer to go through several menus to find a herbal remedy for their malady, freeing up the time of the shop staff in busy periods. The only problem with this was that the ghost had learned to use it too.

My wife Jo was using the computer to look for a herbal remedy for a chest cough. The screen was flickering a lot and then a message bar at the bottom suddenly presented a message to her, as if she'd typed it in while searching the database. The message read, 'Hello I'm dead'. My wife

The Wicker Herbal in Surrey Street today.

brought me over to show me the message and I asked her if she'd typed it in herself, to which she replied, no, she couldn't have done because the screen clears each time a new page appears, as does the message bar. We left the area where the computer was sitting and went to leave the shop with the message still on the screen. As we were leaving a member of staff called to us and asked if we were having trouble with it, to which my wife replied, 'No, but someone's having fun communicating with us through it'. The older shop staff smiled and said, 'More trouble than it's worth that thing. It just flicks through pages by itself even though it's supposed to shut down after a few minutes. Thing is there's no one around when it does it.' I looked at my wife and we decided to leave the staff in peace with the ghost.

The Brown Bear Public House (Norfolk Street)

This old brick building used to be the first Sheffield Library, it was built from local brick and as such, it's suffering today from erosion and frost damage. However, the inhabitant we're going to talk about now is from its days as a public house in the mid-Victorian times. The Brown Bear pub was a popular place to go to when this area was filled with small theatres and fun houses. It had a good clientele and an even better reputation. The Brown Bear even ran a coaching service from its premises for those who were too drunk or too afraid to step out into Sheffield's dark streets after hours.

Now the ghost that still haunts The Brown Bear was the old coachman called James who did the runs in the evening. He would take the drunken revellers home and return for the next batch until the pub was empty. The thing he liked about his job was that he was his own man, he never had to ask when and where he had to go as he knew the routes and the clientele and was often rewarded for getting them home safely. His problems began one night when he was taking a fully laden coach out on a dark, wet night. The roads weren't surfaced as they are today and the coach fell into a pothole, dislodging him from the driver's seat and throwing him under the wheels of the coach. He was lucky that the coach only rolled over his legs but that was bad enough and the passengers helped him into the coach and took him back to The Brown Bear.

When they arrived a physician was sent for from the medical school just up the road from the pub. He saw the condition of the breaks in his legs and told the landlord that he'd never be able to drive the coaching stock again. The coachman was in great pain and asked for his wife but his wife was nowhere to be seen in the rooms they shared above the public house. Unknown to him, she was accustomed to seeing a well-to-do pub regular while he worked. When she finally arrived home she found her husband bedridden and with little prospect of ever working again. When later he learned of wife's adultery the arguments rang out through the entire pub. He tried to cajole her into staying with him at least while his legs healed but she argued that he wasn't a coachman anymore, his legs weren't healing and he'd be a cripple for the rest of his life. She 'deserved better than that'. Over the weeks it became clear to him that he'd lost her to the rich man she was seeing. When he was finally able to walk a short distance without help she left him for the richer life she craved. Her lover offered her an apartment on Bank Street if she'd be his mistress; she accepted and left with everything she owned in a Gladstone bag. The last words he shouted after her were said to be, 'You'll be back, when he realises you can't cook and you nag, you'll be back'.

The landlord wasn't a man without a heart and offered him a choice of new jobs, a cellarman's position or a barman. The cellarman paid more but it involved heavy lifting but the coachman jumped at the chance of the job. He'd be able to do his work when he wanted as long as the cellar never ran dry. He accepted the job and set to work that day. After a week of struggling he finally admitted to the landlord that the work was too much for his legs to cope with and took the barman's job instead. Now all was well for a while until people began to tell him about the beauty his wife had become – that she'd filled out, dressed in silks and rode in coaches. It was all too much for him and he fell into a deep depression. He worked as well as he could but his legs were weak and he was more of a burden than a help to the landlord.

It came to a head when he saw her pass by with her new lover and he was heard to say to the landlord that he was going to check on the brew tun and see if the crates were ready to be brought up for the evening trade. The landlord didn't think anything of it and went on serving. A few hours later he begin to wonder where his barman had gone and went looking for him.

The Brown Bear pub where James the coachman hanged himself and then returned to haunt his employer.

He found him hanging from a rafter in the brewhouse above the brewing tun. He'd wrapped a rope around the beam and hanged himself, one boot gently tapping the brew tun, the other kicked off in his struggle to end his own life.

Now we move forward to 1985 where The Brown Bear was being managed by a relief manager called Mr John Conroy. He'd been brought in to replace the old manager who had to leave suddenly. The reason for his departure was to reveal itself to Mr Conroy soon enough. After a long evening of work and a full pub, Mr Conroy decided to count up the takings upstairs in the office at the top of the pub. Going upstairs he made sure the doors were bolted shut, the alarm was on downstairs and he was alone in the pub. Settling down with a glass of brandy and his work he set to counting up the takings and staff wages. He was halfway through when he heard footsteps coming up the stairs to the first floor. Knowing he was alone, Mr Conroy put it down to the building settling itself after the warm night and the heavy traffic passing it and carried on. After a few moments the footsteps occurred again, this time on the landing outside the office and approaching the door. Mr Conroy flew up out of his chair and opened the door, expecting

The Brown Bear pub in Norfolk Street.

to meet a burglar or a member of staff who'd got locked in by mistake. To his amazement there was nothing there, not even a breeze, only the dark of the stairway and the small landing. A little shaken Mr Conroy went back to his task and tried to put the sounds down to the buildings next door. He didn't get very far as the door flew open and the sound of a limping man came into the room! Mr Conroy shovelled the money into the safe and flew down the stairs and out into the night.

The next morning, feeling a little braver but still worried, he returned to work and as he approached the front doors noticed one of the cleaning ladies waiting for him to open up. The older women noticed he seemed reluctant to enter but said nothing until she'd finished her work for the day when she approached him and asked him why he was so nervous. He then recounted the tale of the night before. She just nodded and looked him over asking, 'Did he do anything else to you?' Mr Conroy was put out at the question and asked her why she'd asked that. The old woman then said, 'You know the reason you're here don't you? Why the last landlord had to leave in such a hurry?' Mr Conroy shook his head; the brewery hadn't told him why, they'd just sent him there. The old cleaning woman smiled and filled him in – the old landlord had been driven out by the ghost of the old coachman. It appeared the ghost disliked him and would make his life miserable; he'd push staff members, he'd move beer down the bar and spill it on customers and he'd pull chairs out from under people. He even tried to push the landlord down the stairs on more than one occasion and was always going into the office on the top floor and messing it up. The cleaner told Mr Conroy that the coachman probably felt he had every right to be up there as they used to be his rooms when he'd been alive.

The coachman is still active in The Brown Bear pub today. He appears to wait until he has a large audience and then objects go missing, beer is spilled and pints have been seen to drift mysteriously down the bar of their own accord to end up before other customers still waiting to be served. The site of the old brew house where the coachman died is now a small beer garden at the back of the pub and on summer evenings people sit outside enjoying the summer breezes unaware of the events that took place here long ago. It is reported, however, that there is one spot in the beer garden that never gets warm, even when the sun has been on it all day. Could this also be the legacy of that unfortunate coachman?

The Graduate Public House (Surrey Street)

This building looks like it should have more than its fair share of ghosts; in late Georgian/early Victorian times it was the Masonic Lodge of Sheffield. The architecture of the building is very unusual and is worth more than a cursory glance, but it's the occupant inside we're interested in. The Graduate used to be called The Surrey and Fringe and it was well known for its student and theatre clientele at one time. Although there was one visitor that not everyone got to see; only bar staff who stayed after midnight had this privilege!

The strange visitor here is a woman dressed in black who walks about on a floor level that is no longer in place – one that was lower than the one they use today. When she appears she is seen with her knees below the level of the floor and her progress is slow and stately as she moves across the now modern kitchen and then goes out through a wall. She's been seen on many occasions by staff and was even questioned by one student worker who asked her what she was doing there. As he approached her she just faded away leaving him dumbfounded and

Surrey Street looking towards the Town Hall.

shaking. The now landlord of The Graduate hasn't seen her himself but many of his staff still refuse to be on the premises after midnight which makes staffing the pub a little difficult with the new licensing laws.

The Town Hall

Plans for Sheffield's new Town Hall were completed in 1889 and the building was eventually finished in 1896 after much deliberation and argument. A building of such grandeur and gothic style might be expected to have ghosts to its name and indeed there have been reports but these seem to have been confined mainly to the lowly kitchens used by Town Hall staff when they need a break. The ghost that lives there makes a nuisance of himself by turning on kettles when

17

Sheffield's grand Town Hall, where the great and the good make decisions that shape the future of the city; a ghostly resident in the back kitchen has his own ideas.

no one is there and letting them boil dry. Kettles have even been seen to boil dry even when the cut-off switch has operated. More of a nuisance is when he decides to throw things around in the kitchen. An impressive example of this took place one afternoon just after the kitchen had been cleaned up for the day and left in order. When an office worker looked in before leaving for home she found the entire place covered in sugar, dried milk, tea bags and coffee, which were scattered everywhere. Angry at the mess she went around the offices trying to find out who'd wrecked the room but found no one who had seen anything. She even asked the nearby security staff but they had not seen anyone entering the room at that time. On reflection one did remember hearing someone in there but had assumed they'd just missed seeing them go in or out. She took them inside to see the damage the ghost had wrought and they helped to clean the mess up. Exactly why the ghost had done this has remained a mystery, but needless to say, not many people talk about the ghost: maybe they don't want to clean up after it.

Leader House (Surrey Street)

Leader House is one of the oldest private houses in Sheffield and was built in 1780 for Thomas Leader who was one of the first silver platers of the city. The ghost that inhabits this house is though,t to be a chambermaid from earlier days. An unusual thing about her is that she's also been seen outside the building she haunts, walking the streets heading towards it and appearing in front of The Graduate pub as a grey misty figure with no face, but dressed in a servant's uniform. She was seen recently by a Novotel worker as he was going to his early morning shift at the hotel, only a short distance away from Leader House.

The ghost appears to think she's still employed at the house. Much to the surprise of the present staff there. In the late 1970s Mrs Edith Mosely was employed to work as a cleaner and at her interview she was asked a rather unusual question, 'Did she believe in the supernatural and did she have a nervous disposition?' She answered 'no' to both questions and got the job. The old maid, however, didn't seem to appreciate the help Mrs Mosely was giving her as many times when she went to clean the offices she would find herself being pestered by her predecessor, blowing cold winds on her face or repeatedly turning off the vacuum cleaner. Mrs Mosely, being of stout heart and no-nonsense Yorkshire stock, asked her once if she wanted to do anything else to her or would she let her get on with her work? The maid blew on her again and Mrs Mosely replied, 'Is that all? Well I've got work to do' and carried on.

Mrs Mosely might have been able to cope with the ghostly maids antics but not everyone has such iron in their blood. When the building changed hands to the Sheffield Development office so did the cleaning staff and the maid got a few new targets to practice her skills on. The new cleaners were much more nervous of her and sometimes refused to clean without someone else to accompany them; the porter's dog refused to go into one room of the building and sometimes barking and snarling at 'nothing' on the stairs in the centre of the property.

The most recent incident occurred when the building was handed over to the Millennium Gallery for its archive and offices in 2001. An employee of the gallery was doing some filing in an upstairs room when the door slammed shut on her and the large cabinets began to shudder and shake. Upset, she managed to get the door open and ran screaming down the stairs to be met by the porter who asked her what had happened. Badly shaken, she was taken back to the gallery, given a cup of tea and again asked to explain what had happened. She refused to go into details except to say that 'a maid had been there'.

In future she asked to have someone with her whenever she went into the archive and for a while things calmed down, until one day in early September 2001 she had again to visit the archives and on entering the door to the room, followed by the porter just behind her, the door slammed shut and locked itself, leaving the archivist inside and the porter outside. The porter heard the sound of screaming and a noise like someone falling down behind the door as he tried to get the door open. After a few moments the door opened to reveal the archivist lying on the floor, rolled into a ball and crying. The archivist refused to enter the building again and was offered a different position working somewhere else. One wonders why the maid disliked this woman enough to scare her away – perhaps she triggered the replaying of events that led to her own death? Porters now use the archive more than the staff and on cold nights it's reported that you can see the ghostly figure of the maid watching out of the large bay window that looks onto the Central Library. She's been seen by students on their way to Hallam University, although most believe it's a dummy in the window but it isn't, it's the ghost of the maid still doing her work!

Above and opposite: *Leader House in Surrey Street, where a ghostly housemaid still goes to work*

Central Library (Surrey Street)

This building is Sheffield's one and only piece of Art Deco Monumentalist architecture. It was built in 1924-5 and was completed on the old site of the medical school which used to house the mortuary slabs that are now in residence at The Wicker Herbal. The following story was given to us as we walked The Steel City Ghost Tour last year by a woman who works in the Central Library in the stacks below the street level where the mortuary used to be.

She described to us the lower stacks where old documents and locked sections are kept. She often works alone down there and is quite used to the peace and quiet but this experience has made her nervous of being alone down there. She'd been restacking a shelf at chest height when she felt something touch her skirt: thinking she'd knocked a book loose she looked down to see a pale arm reaching out at her through the solid books. The hand was opening and closing in supplication and she watched in stunned silence while the hand twitched and shuddered on the arm, then fell limp and faded out, leaving the bookcase as it had been before. Shocked, she

Leader House today.

The Medical School in Surrey Street, now the site of the Central Library.

stood in silence for a little while then moved away from the area still keeping her eyes on the place the arm had appeared. The arm has never appeared again but there have been reports of sounds like a dying breath heard in the stacks below the main library and many staff members now go below in pairs.

Perhaps the ghost is that of a man brought into the medical school for dissection who was not yet dead. It is thought that this was not an uncommon occurrence in the days when corpses were bought for research with not too many questions asked about their origins. Some of these unfortunates were opened on the cold marble slab only to die under the mortician's scalpel. Perhaps the library staff are still feeling the presence of a victim of this nefarious practice today!

The basement book stacks at the Central Library where strange noises and a grabbing hand have broken the peace.

Sheffield Central Library today.

The Lyceum Theatre (Tudor Street)

This theatre has not one but three ghosts! Sheffield seems to have a propensity for having more than its fair share of ghosts and no other theatre in Sheffield has the variety or character of the inhabitants of the Lyceum once described as 'A Stradivarius of Theatres'. Designed by W.G. Sprague it provides an unobstructed view of the stage from any seat inside the theatre, a claim of paramount importance for any theatre, both then and now. When the Lyceum was opened on Boxing Day 1893, it was to great acclaim and over two thousand people attending the opening night. One of the ghosts belongs to an earlier structure that used to occupy the ground where the Lyceum stands today.

Before the Lyceum there was a building called The Grand Theatre of Varieties, a large wooden structure which staged all kinds of entertainments, from acrobats to plays and animal acts. A ghost

The Lyceum Theatre today.

who appears to come from this period is a large gentle giant of a man called 'Ben'. He is most usually reported near the stage doors but has also been seen in the front of the Lyceum, talking to the customers. There's an oddity about Ben: he smells! He apparently has a somewhat earthy odour of horses and animals and it's been reported that he asks about the city newspapers and scandal sheets, wondering who is in the news or what has happened recently. He once asked how the queen was doing and the man talking to him replied that he didn't take much interest in the royals. Ben apparently looked disturbed and then asked him how the empire was going instead; the man, curious at such a question, stopped and looked back towards Ben only to find that he had completely disappeared. Ben is always apparently accompanied by the scent of horses and is dressed in dark overalls, large boots and a cap. A gentle ghost, he appears presumably to check up on the place where he used to work and to see what's happening in the city he knew.

Another ghost of the Lyceum is one that takes his work very seriously and expects everyone else to as well. When the Lyceum went into decline in the 1970s, it was left derelict and empty for a good few years until 1981 when it was reopened as a venue for rock concerts. To be used as such it needed rewiring and several electricians were employed for the task. The building was locked during the work to ensure the safety of the public and prevent anyone wandering inside to see what was going on. Locked in, the gang split up to do the job and one day, when it came to lunchtime, one of the lads seemed irritated and upset. The foreman asked the lad what was the matter and he told him someone had been watching him all day. He described a man dressed in a straw boater hat, flannel trousers, striped jacket, handlebar moustache and carrying a cane. He thought one of the other workers was taking the micky out of him and he told them to 'Bugger off' and to leave him alone. The man still stood there watching him work and only left when he'd finally finished the job. The foreman looked a little pale when he answered the young man and told him he'd described the old manager of the Lyceum. The man was a stickler for good craftsmanship and wouldn't trust anyone to do a job that was important without him overlooking the work.

The old theatre manager has also been seen by stage hands today; he's been known to rearrange props and items on stage, even in the middle of a play, if he's unhappy with them. If you go to the Lyceum be on the lookout for a straw boater appearing in the wings, it might be the old manager.

The third story is the most tragic; it concerns the jilted lover of an actor from the D'Oyly Carte Company. The woman in question came to the theatre to watch the company's version of *The Lady in Black*. She took the centre seat in the first balcony and immediately fell for the leading actor. He also spied her and it was said it was love at first sight. After the performance she was ushered to the back of the theatre and met the star and struck up a relationship with him. Over the three-month run of the play she came to every performance and the stagehands got used to letting her into the backstage early so she could wait for her love. The local papers and scandal sheets were reporting the success of the play and of the love affair it had spawned and conversations hummed and buzzed about what would happen when the troupe moved on. The actor and the young woman lived for nothing else but each other while they were there, so she fully expected him to ask her to go with him when the company moved on but there was a problem. The reviews had been so good that his own self worth had exploded and the next city they were heading for had better prospects than Sheffield. The last night came and there wasn't a ticket left in the city; the love affair as well as the play were in people's minds. More than once the young woman was made to feel the attention and stares of the crowd around her as the play went on stage. She left early and waited for him in the number one dressing room; champagne and flowers were everywhere.

After the last curtain call, it took him nearly twenty minutes to get to the dressing room where she was waiting for him. She was wearing a grey silk dress that brought out her colouring, the door was open to the hallway and many people were crowded around the door hoping to hear the declarations of love and proposal of marriage that everyone had been waiting for – but it was not to be. The actor spurned his young love, telling her he was leaving alone, his star was rising and would 'do better' in the next city. Heartbroken she ran from the room, upsetting the champagne and smashing it to the floor, the sound of the crowds ringing in her ears as she left the theatre.

The play, and the actor, moved on, but his lady still came to the theatre, perhaps hoping that he'd return. The stage hands and ushers were quiet in their handling of her but the theatre clientele weren't so sensitive. She became a subject of ridicule, a lesson and a joke for mothers to warn their daughters about. After a few months of this she decided her life had become too much to bear. Entering the empty theatre one day she made her way to her usual seat and taking a rope from the backstage she secured it to the balcony from where she'd first seen her love.

The Lyceum theatre where a lady in grey once lost her heart to an actor. Betrayed and spurned she hanged herself from the balcony and haunts the theatre to this day.

Tying the other end around her neck, she dropped off the edge. She was found by stagehands later that day, taken down and buried by her family. The ghost of The Grey Lady still walks the hallways and backstage of the theatre. She has been heard crying and running down the backstage and the sound of a smashing bottle is often heard in the number one dressing room. She's even been seen sitting in her favourite seat in the balcony; a couple watching the latest production of *The Lady In Black* told us of this fascinating sighting. The woman of the couple had been very impressed by the costume of the woman sitting to her right and nudged her partner to tell him about it but when she turned back the woman had gone. The dress material she said was a beautiful dove grey, old-fashioned but not Victorian in style, and she thought the woman had been staring sadly at the stage.

The Roxy Nightclub (Arundel Gate)

This is a tale of a modern-day impressario and lothario who owned and operated the Roxy Nightclub which became a haven for the revellers of Sheffield and outlying towns and cities. He died in the 1980s but apparently went back to work, to the place he'd loved as a mortal soul.

This tale was told to us by an ex-doorman and odd-job man of the Roxy called Wesley. Now Wesley is not a man given to flights of fancy or a man likely to lie about what he sees or experiences. He was once asked to go up into the lighting rig at the Roxy to check it for faults because it had been coming on when there was no obvious power going to it. As he went up the ladder he was surprised to see a full pint of beer and a lit cigarette drifting about above the empty club, towards the VIP area. He was so shocked he let go of the ladder and almost fell to the dance floor below. Regaining his balance Wesley climbed down and went to look for someone to ask if there was anyone else up there as well as him. He found another member of staff and asked him if there was anyone else up on the VIP level. 'No', he said, there was no one else in yet – only him and Wesley. Wesley told him about the floating pint and the cigarette on the VIP floor, to which he was told that it was probably just the old owner, who had always liked to 'feather his love nest before the young ladies came in'.

This wasn't the only 'presence' that the club noticed after he had died. As owner he had always done a good job of 'meeting and greeting' the customers to his club but was also notorious for patting the occasional behind of the young female customers, especially if they were wearing short skirts and dresses! When he died they had to find someone else who would do the 'front of house' job that he was so good at. They found a replacement in a young man called Simon. He soon settled into the job but then he too appeared to be taking advantage of the female customers, much as his predecessor appeared to have done. After a few instances of this, he was asked to refrain from doing it but Simon claimed he had no idea what they were talking about. He was moved out of the job but that didn't stop the women being patted! The old owner, it seems, had come back to touch the ladies, occasionally slapping his bar staff as well as one lady called Joyce found out to her surprise! Thinking it was Simon she turned to give him a piece of her mind, to find there was no one there. There were other strange happenings; internal telephones would ring with no one on the other end and the swing doors between bars would open and close on their own.

The club building was later taken over by St Thomas's church for a while, until he began to make his presence felt with the ladies of the congregation. He'd slap them on the rear too as they passed his spot so women would enter by a different door. On one occasion after a service on the way out a large slap rang out and the priest turned to his flock and apologised for the ghost! The church moved out soon afterwards and it is now planned to turn the building into a 169-room hotel. We wonder if the ghost will love the chambermaids as much as he loved the members of his old club?

The Roxy Nightclub where women used to dance under the fond gaze of its proprietor. After he died many of his young female customers 'felt' sure he had returned.

Chapel Walk

This street is included here because of the many former city residents who now lie just two feet below its pavement. Chapel Walk is a survivor of ancient Sheffield. The pattern of the streets have changed over time but the ground underneath here has more bodies buried under it than any other piece of ground in the city centre. The bodies that lay under this road date back to the earliest settlement and the establishment of the cathedral; no ghosts have actually been spotted here but there have been some unsubstantiated tales of people being grabbed by the ankles as they walk down there at night. We await more reports so until then it may just be a piece of historical whimsy!

Chapel Walk today.

Bodies lie only just below the surface here in Chapel Walk seen here in earlier times.

Boots the Chemist in Fargate, c. 1938. A gentleman in a top hat and dark coat haunts the shop floors and has been alarming the staff here for decades.

Boots the Chemist (Fargate Branch)

Boots the Chemist has been in this building on this site in Fargate since 1933. Several older buildings were pulled down to build this shop. The ghost of Boots seems to reside in the cellars of the building but in recent years has also been seen on the ground floor. Shop cashiers have seen him walking the shop floor and emerging from the lift that goes to every floor of the building. When it appears it manifests as a man dressed in a top hat, dark coat and cape and carrying a cane. He walks out of the lift, across the shop floor and out through a wall.

Now this ghost sounds quite calm and quiet now but his antics were once anything but that. When he first began his campaign of haunting he started on the shop girls of the newly opened Boots store in 1933. The girls would go and collect stock from the cellar and bring it back to the shop floor via Black Swan Walk (a small side street) because the cellar didn't have an opening to the main shop at that point. They would always go in pairs because of the ghost's habit of slamming the door shut and barring it from reopening again. Lights would also turn themselves

33

Boots in Fargate where a ghost uses the service lift.

off while they were down there, leaving the girls in darkness. The ghost kept up its campaign of terror throughout the war years but went strangely quiet from the 1950s till the early 1980s, when a new stores man was taken on, Mr Allison.

Mr Allison's run in with the ghost consisted of two incidents; the first encounter had him being attacked by a large sack of flour that had been put on shelving in the alleyway that led to the cellar. The company used the alleyway as an extra storage place for stock and as Mr Allison passed the shelving, he heard the door slam shut to the alleyway and a 'paf' sound. Turning to look behind him he saw the sack of flour on the stone floor and decided to check the other sacks of flour, to see if they were stacked properly. They were laid eighteen inches away from the edge of the shelving. The sack had landed and burst over five feet away from the shelves, so had travelled nearly seven feet. If he'd been walking more slowly it would have hit him in the neck. A little perturbed Mr Allison cleaned up the mess and carried on with his duties, telling the head porter about the accident later. He was rewarded with the news from the older man that he had always felt uneasy in the cellar on his own, as if he was disturbing some awful act that he'd just walked in on, and as such, he rarely went into the cellar alone.

His second encounter was more vicious. Mr Allison had just finished putting some stock on the shelving in the alleyway when a piece of properly stored glass flew off a shelf. The pane flew off at the level of his neck; if he'd been any slower in walking forward the pane would have caused him a nasty and possibly fatal injury. It was the last straw for Mr Allison, who went back upstairs to tell the staff, and some gathering customers, that he wasn't going back down into that cellar because a ghost was trying to kill him. Mr Allison became very exuberant in his exchanges with the floor manager who refused to believe him. Mr Allison left soon after the exchange and never returned to the premises.

The ghost had driven off one store man but he wasn't the first to come a cropper at the store. A part-time security guard and night watchman also had a very odd run in with the ghost of the cellar. The man used an Alsatian dog, trained for security work, which had saved his life on several occasions and successfully seen off robbers trying to break into the store. The man used a regular route which took him down Black Swan Walk to check the outer door and the cellar before returning to the shop floor and the upper floors. He took this route at least three times a night but on one occasion as he was going down Black Swan Walk his dog began to whimper. Ignoring the dog, he carried on his route into the alleyway and storage that led to the cellars. But he never made it to the end. His dog dropped to all fours, whimpered and took off, pulling the watchman with him. The dog was so spooked by the occurrence that the watchman went and barricaded himself and his dog inside the offices above the store, choosing not to leave until daylight. He was so upset by the incident that he took early retirement soon afterwards.

The ghost continued to play tricks on staff and members of the public until finally the management decided to have a look at the cellars to put an to end the rumours about the haunting. An old tunnel was discovered that led from the back of the cellar to the cathedral. One man walked the tunnel in its entirety and found the other end blocked up. It was decided to brick up the entrance to the tunnel and it was eventually sealed off in early 1986. Soon after this time McDonalds were opening a restaurant nearby and wanted to extend their own cellars to open up a basement floor. They approached their cellar neighbours and Boots sold them the part of their own cellar with the blocked up tunnel entrance. For a while everything was calm and quiet as McDonalds now had the ghost in their space but it wasn't to last: the ghost moved back through after a few months and began causing trouble again in Boots' part of the cellar!

Boots in Fargate where strange things happen in the cellars.

The ghost is still active in the shop and we've been told by the girls who work there that the store still has its regular spectral visitor. He now uses the new lift that was installed a few years ago. Staff have seen the same gentleman dressed in long coat and top hat come out of the lift and walk to the right, straight through a wall, then re-appear twenty minutes later and go back down again using the lift. Some girls have seen the lift being called down to the cellar and reappear with unwanted stock in the middle of the day when the stores man isn't even in the cellar, and when he appears he wonders why there is spare stock on the shop floor in the middle of the day!

The ghost also had a surprise in store for a lady manager who related her own personal tale to me about her experience with the ghost. She'd been woken at 2 a.m. by the police because the store alarms were going off and she was the registered key holder for the alarm system. She drove into the centre of town and found the police car waiting for her with two police officers. One stayed outside of the shop while the other went in with her and they went to see what had caused the alarm to go off. Searching through the store for signs of a break-in, they found nothing unusual save a half mannequin on the floor, which was being used, for an advertising display. Picking up the mannequin they secured it back in place and shook the shelving just to be sure that it wouldn't fall off and set off the internal alarm again. Satisfied they walked away from the shelving only to have the mannequin fly off the shelf and hit them both solidly in the back before coming to rest on the floor. Needless to say they were both disturbed by the incident and left the premises, leaving the alarm switched off for the night. Ever since this event the manageress has refused to go into the store alone as she believes the ghost doesn't like her.

What the connection might be between this building and its blocked-off tunnel, the cathedral and the ghostly man in the top hat can only be speculation but the hauntings have gone on for a long number of years and have involved a large number of people over that time. No doubt we will hear of more strange events at this store in the years to come.

Novotel Hotel (Arundel Gate)

The ghost that haunts this building truly is international; the ghost is thought to be of a German tourist who died on the fifth floor of the hotel. His ghost is said to turn on the television in the rooms of the fifth floor looking for something interesting to watch or to get attention from the guests or staff working the hotel.

Several chambermaids have felt his presence up there while they've been cleaning and on more than one occasion they've seen his shadow pass them as they've been cleaning. Floor five is the quietest floor but it also seems to be the coldest; whether it's because of their unpaying guest we're not sure but he's still there flicking through the channels.

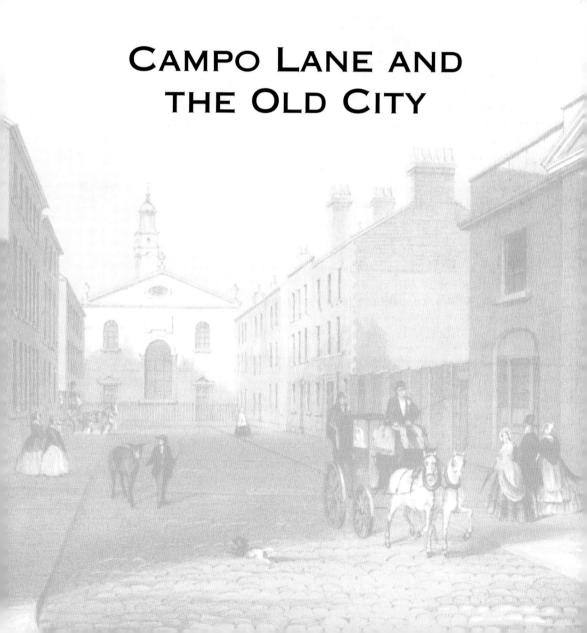

TWO

CAMPO LANE AND THE OLD CITY

CAMPO LANE AND
THE OLD CITY

Sheffield Cathedral

The cathedral we see in Sheffield today is the result of many additions and changes over the centuries and it is haunted by ghosts from its past that inhabit and play with the structure of the old building.

Our first ghoulish story takes place outside the cathedral on the site of an old graveyard when the Supertram tracks were being laid over the old Victorian ones in 1994. What was discovered one hot Friday afternoon horrified two workmen and those working around them. They were digging the foundations for the tram stop when one workman's pickaxe went through something he thought was wood but he brought out what looked to be a freshly buried arm. His workmate did one better by uncovering a head with hair and flesh still on it. Badly shocked, they called the alarm and the police arrived. For seven hours, the centre of Sheffield came to a standstill as experts worked out exactly where these bodies had come from; were they recent burials of unfortunate murder victims?

It turned out that the bodies were actually from the early 1500s and were most likely plague or Black Death victims because the burial site wasn't marked or previously known. The reason the bodies were still partially fleshed has something to do with a peculiarity of Sheffield soils, being mostly a mix of heavy clays and sediment with bacteria levels so low that decomposition of bodies is very slow. This would explain why these bodies were still in a recognisable shape when they were unearthed by the digging of the foundations. They were excavated and retrieved by Arcus, the Sheffield University Archaeology Department, and then later reburied by the diocese.

The first ghost tale is of a maid, dressed in Elizabethan clothing, her mantle of a deep solid colour and her head covered in a simple but decorative style. She has been observed walking in front of the rood screen on Sundays and has been seen by one man on several occasions. Her pace is serene and calm as if she has all the time in the world. On one occasion this man was sitting with a friend in his usual spot, two rows back from the rood screen, when his friend grabbed hold of his arm tightly and he noticed where she was looking. They watched the ghost pass by the front of the screen on her way out of the church by a separate door. They both watched her leave and return to the service. He still takes his pew every Sunday and gives a prayer for the lady he sees glide by. Some have speculated that the woman could be the ghost of Queen Mary who was imprisoned in Sheffield for a while but the lady who is seen here is a young girl not a woman in her middle age. Whoever she is, her ghost seems to be a welcome one to the parishioners.

The next ghost is a little mischief maker who loves to play with the electric lights in the cathedral. When the church is locked up for the night it's often the case that when they come back to open up in the morning, the lights will be burning again. It got the a point where the diocese said if the lights turned themselves on when the curate had left and had looked back to check if the lights were off they were to leave them alone. Before this they would go back open up, turn off the alarm, turn out the lights, turn the alarm back on, lock up and walk away, only to see the lights turn back on again. After a few times of doing this the curate complained to the diocese and the edict was given to leave the ghost to its play.

Another trick it plays is with the candles that the faithful light for prayers for their sick and loved ones. One such incident occured when a lady who was a regular at the cathedral was lighting a candle to her loved ones who'd died in the war. When it blew out in front of her eyes, she assumed it had been her breath that had done it and she went to relight it but it relit itself in front of her. Then the other candles began to go out all down the cathedral until only hers was alight, then they all relit themselves again – her prayers were more fervent after this!

There is another ghost that resides in the Chapel of Saint George, one who loves to move the regimental flags as if there is a breeze running through the cathedral. It has been speculated that this could be the sixth Earl of Shrewsbury who was the gaoler of Mary Queen of Scots when she was here in Sheffield. He was a fighting man himself and raised several regiments for the defence of England when he was alive.

The area where the cathedral now stands, it has been speculated, was a meeting place for the pre-Christian residents of Sheffield. The Saxon cross that was found on the site of the cathedral is one of a kind and now resides in the British Museum. It holds pagan iconography as well as Christian, as if the residents were hedging their bets about the area they lived in, as if the old gods were still listening outside in the forest that surrounded the first wooden church. Nowadays there is little left of the pagan past but there are a couple of interesting sculptures on the ceiling of the church. Over the font is a green man head, which has been said to wink at women who stand to the left of the font and look up. Also in the Lady Chapel is a Sheela-Na-Gig who smiles beneficently on all who pass under her golden gaze, a symbol of fertility and wealth; the spirit of fecundity brought into God's house to provide benefit for the faithful. The cathedral itself has been worked on over many centuries and is an architectural anomaly, a mixture of styles and reworking over the centuries. Even now it appears some of its faithful return to light a candle, or to say a prayer, even though they've been dead for centuries.

Campo Lane

Campo Lane was a boundary of Sheffield for a very long time, the last road before the moors and the cathedral. The lane itself has been used for over six hundred years and in its time has seen many changes and a few notable deaths. The tales of Campo Lane are varied, but we'll start with the oldest, the Barghast of Campo Lane.

Our tale begins in the 1750s with a man who worked at a public house (believed to have been called The Osbourne House) on the far end of Campo Lane and Hartshead (a street in those days and not a square). The man was lame and walked with the support of crutches and one night when he was walking down Campo Lane to his home in Gregory Row he saw a large hound padding silently toward him. Lifting his lantern he saw its large eyes and noticed the dark coat of the hound reflected no light, neither from his lantern nor the moon above. Recognising the beast to be a Barghast, the hound of death, he quickly made for Hick's stile, now the entrance to Paradise Square from Campo Lane. Having climbed over the stile he slowed his pace through the field as he believed the hound could not cross a man-made object and believed he was safe.

Turning to look back he was frightened to see the beast leap upon the stile and jump into the field after him. The Barghast brings bad luck or sudden death to any man he touches and he did his utmost to get away from the approaching beast. Just then his crutch found a rabbit hole and he went down in the field. He pushed himself back up and set off again, eventually reaching home where his wife had already locked up for the night; hammering on the door he broke the lock and told his wife what was behind him. She took up a broom and a handful of salt and waited for the beast to appear: when it rounded the corner it came up short and stopped dead when it saw her. It stayed still for a few moments then padded away; a Barghast will not attack a woman. The hound returned to the lane and the man went to bed with his wife, but from that day on he never needed his crutches, for the hound had taken away his lameness.

Curiously, tradition has it that Barghasts may even protect women from harm. There is a tale from Outibridge of an elderly woman coming home late at night who was escorted by a ghostly hound, the size of a small pony, on her way home along a dangerous road. The footpads who frequented the route avoided her because of the dog that turned 'great eyes like lamps on coaches' toward them when they shifted in the darkness. These are old tales but does the Barghast still haunt Sheffield?

In 1999 there was a curious incident that suggests the hound may have appeared again, this time to two students near the Botanical Gardens. Duncan and Will were walking home from a night out when Duncan was attacked by a large dog that ran off and then disappeared into thin air as it crossed the road! Although there were no wounds to be seen at first, as time passed, rake marks from the dog's claws could be seen, as could bite marks on his skin. Although the student recovered physically from his ordeal after a good night's sleep he was so troubled by the incident that he abandoned his studies soon afterwards.

Now we move onto another dog, or hounds, story, based on a legend that goes far back into history. 'The Hounds of Gabriel' are a terrifying pack of hounds that come to chase and collect sinners to take them to Hell. In 1861 a Mr Holland was sufficiently frightened by the ghostly sounds of howling beasts as he walked home past the Sheffield Parish Church one night that he believed he had actually heard them!

In legend these hounds were supposed to be the size of Shetland ponies, with white fur and red ears, able to run faster than a horse and stand on two legs like a man. The hounds chased after sinners, and the soon to be dead, led by a rider mounted on a large horse of dappled grey or pure white. The rider carried a human thighbone holding a parchment of flesh with the names of the 'dead' to be collected on it. The hounds were known as Gabriel's because in Christian tradition he is the angel of death who claims human souls that are unworthy to be condemned.

The tradition probably goes back further and may originally have involved the pagan god Awarn, ruler of the dead lands and the winter months. He was said to ride with his hounds to collect the souls of those about to die. With full medieval gruesomeness their habits are described: the hounds chase their victims and when caught they crack open the chest and remove and consume the beating heart, as the soul was thought to reside there. They also consumed the head

Campo Lane where some believe the 'Hounds of Gabriel' hunt in the dark hours.

Campo Lane, one of Sheffield's oldest thoroughfares, where the 'Black Shuck', or Barghast, pads in search of his next victim.

Campo Lane today.

as it left the body with the last breath! Leaving no trace of the victim's body behind the hounds then returned to the awful rider to regurgitate the soul into a leather bag to be carried to its final destination in another world.

The sound of them hunting is said to be like a pack of foxhounds chasing a fox. We are not sure what to make of claims that such sounds may have been heard in Campo Lane on dark nights! Perhaps the pack still hunts in Sheffield, near the river maybe, awaiting the unwary ... who knows?

In November 2005 two mediums accompanying us on the Sheffield Ghost Tour reported to us afterwards that they'd seen two white hounds with white ears sitting on scaffolding above them both. It was only after hearing this story that they began to reconsider the significance of what they might have seen and both were quite shaken.

The home of the 'Kitchen Ghost' in Campo Lane. She brought about the death of the owner.

The Kitchen Ghost (Campo Lane)

The next tale is of a ghost that actually harmed someone, an apparition that caused the untimely death of a householder on Campo Lane in 1855. The lady in question was coming downstairs into her kitchen, which was in the basement, when she saw a woman in white on the stairs in front of her, which shocked her so much that she fainted dead away. People heard her fall and came to see what the problem was and saw her at the bottom of the stairs as white as a sheet. Dr Fravell, who lived close by, was sent for and attended to her. It appears she'd had a heart attack and so was taken to bed to recover and rest. The ghost, however, was to cause more problems for this household; as news of the 'haunted house' spread it became a sight for many people to visit who would look into the cellar kitchen at all hours of the day and night hoping to see the lady in white. Eventually the lady was well enough to come downstairs but on the very day she did the ghost reappeared to her, and this time it was seen by others too. The shock was too much for her and she collapsed and died in her husband's arms. The ghost was never seen again after this second appearance, as if she'd done her work and was now happy to leave for the paradise she deserved. What reason did this ghost have for appearing here and with such devastating effect?

Paradise Square

Paradise Square is a beautiful Georgian square that was once Hick's Field – where the Barghast chased a man to his front door. The square itself has many beautiful buildings and there is history in the very brickwork of the houses that surround the central area, once a bustling pottery market. Several tales of violence and haunting are linked with this old place and we start with the day the cavalry charged through it.

The square has been used for all kinds of meetings over the years. John Wesley the Methodist preacher often came here, attracting large crowds, and in 1779 he gave a sermon in the square to the largest number of people he had ever preached to on a weekday anywhere.

In the early nineteenth century the Chartist movement was gaining much support in the industrial north with its efforts to gain improvements for working people in the cities. They held a number of meetings in the square over the years, often attracting huge crowds, and in September 1839 one of the largest meetings was dispersed by troops leading to a running battle and a number of arrests. There was panic on the street that day and some injuries amongst those fleeing the mounted charges. Some say it is still possible to hear the horse's hooves clattering over the cobblestones again on a dark night!

A Mrs S. saw these apparitions one day in the early 1990s, coming out of the side alley into Paradise Square. They were dressed in brown wool, a long smock-type dress with no decoration or buttons, a strange hood on their bent heads that only allowed a small amount of their face to be seen. But it was the way they walked that surprised her most of all: they were tied together with collars around their necks like prisoners. All the figures moved silently across the cobbles, fading out after they'd passed the central lamppost, no sound was heard from them but the tapping of a stick on the ground in front of them. She was left with a sense of pain and dread but also a feeling of sickness; her hands had gone to her stomach and were rubbing it until she noticed the women had faded away. Who were these poor women and where were they going? What event from the past did it represent?

When Paradise Square became a place for lawyers and court business the local tavern or gin mills became a little more upmarket. One of the most rowdy was called the 'Q in the Corner', a gin mill with a diverse clientele and a blind fiddle player called Stephen. He was known throughout Sheffield for his skill and ability to play any tune once started by someone whistling. It is said that people even came from as far away as Bradford to hear him play and he often filled the square with strains of beautiful music and laughter. The old gin mill has long since been lost but Blind Stephen still plays his music for the residents of Paradise Square. His violin has often been heard on a summer's evening playing a jaunty tune, but never anything modern. The offices that now fill his old quarters are still used and they report that Blind Stephen still plays his tunes occasionally but not as often now as he used to do. Many a day's work has been lightened by the strains of music coming from his ghostly fiddle.

Above: Paradise Square has seen many dramatic events and harbours the odd ghost as well. It is seen here in 1883.
Opposite: Paradise Square in 1887 with crowds celebrating Queen Victoria's Jubilee.

The Penny Doctor of St Peter's Close

This next tale is not for the faint of heart, for when this ghost was alive and kicking the words 'doctor' and 'butcher' were sometimes almost synonymous. The building where these hauntings take place is at the back of the 1923 Mazda building that fronts onto Campo Lane, yet the ghosts were here way before this frontage was built. The rear of this building was built much earlier, dating from the early 1830s, when it had a sinister resident who still apparently holds onto his tenancy.

The lady in question who bought the new apartment in the Mazda building after it had been refurbished and completed was quite pleased she'd managed to get hold of the one she'd looked at first, because of the floor. The floor of her now open-plan apartment was half wooden and half unsealed green marble; the only problem was that the marble was stained by what she thought was oil at first. Yet when she washed and scrubbed the floor the water came out brown. It wasn't until she joined one of my city tours and heard what had gone on in this building that she put two and two together. Despite all she still resides in the building but someone else seems to have moved out, but we'll get to that part soon.

When she first moved in to the newly converted apartment she noticed that she sometimes felt uneasy about nothing in particular but could not identify anything specifically that was wrong. It came to a head one night when she was sitting at home watching television when

she heard a woman's scream echo around her flat. Knowing it wasn't her own television she wondered if it was someone else's, but she'd never heard anything from her neighbours before and the walls were thick and soundproof. The only other explanation was that someone was being attacked in the hallway so she went to the door to investigate and looked out. Her gaze was met by nothing but the regular corridor and the images on the walls so she put the scream down to having come from a radio or television somewhere else after all.

About a month later the incident happened again, but this time it wasn't just her who heard it, it was also her neighbours on both sides. They all checked with each other that it wasn't their televisions or someone on their floor; one even went upstairs to check if it was someone above them, but it wasn't. They were a little disturbed but eventually went back to their own apartments and carried on with their evenings.

Paradise Square today.

About one month later yet another scream was heard, this time so loud that it was heard by the entire floor of the building. It echoed around and sounded as if someone was being murdered. Very scared this time they all spent most of the night in one flat only venturing back much later to their own homes.

The next month there was no scream and nothing like it has occurred since but what has been heard instead make the scream even more mysterious. The lady who first heard the screams was one day sitting with her windows open above the small road that runs down the back of St Peter's Close. She heard what sounded like someone messing around with the bins below, or so she thought. Putting her head out of the window she could see the bins but there was no one nearby - nor any sight of an urban fox! What she did hear instead was a conversation between two men, just underneath her window, but when she looked down there was no one there to see. She could also hear what sounded like a cart and horse. The two men appeared to be discussing payments and also about moving something, both talking in a strong Sheffield accent. The voices then stopped and she heard the cart moving off down the street to the end of St Peter's Close and then all went quiet.

Was this woman witness to a ghostly return of the body men, suppliers to the Penny Doctor? The tale of a Penny Doctor and his exploits may be something of an urban myth in Sheffield but some of the story is based in reality. There was a doctor who lived in the chambers of St Peter's Close whose gainful employment we know was not all from the treating of the sick but sometimes also trading as a specimen importer, a medical specimen dealer. He imported anatomy specimens from the assizes of Leeds and Edinburgh. Executed murderers and rapists ended their days in glass jars and this doctor sold them to the medical students of Sheffield. What they didn't know (or maybe some of them did?) is that the specimens weren't always from a legal source.

The doctor had a practice in his rooms that catered for the needs of the community around him; being a 'penny doctor' he ministered for those who couldn't afford the more expensive treatment of other doctors. The poor were his patients and no doubt they often died on his table too with no one or nothing to pay him with. So, it is thought, some of these ended up in bits on his dissection table. He sold to the students around him and he may even have obtained a little extra by letting them help him dismember a body, giving them more experience and helping him to dispose of a patient who had perhaps died a little before his time.

Could this be where the young lady's stained floor came from? Those large dark patches on the green marble, the stains that dot around the floor coloured in brown and black and are difficult to remove. Could they be the blood of the doctor's dismembering room?

From the doctor's own accounts he was quite prosperous and so probably sold many specimens in his residency of St Peter's Close. He also dealt with the ladies of the night, helping them out with their unwanted pregnancies and perhaps also acquiring more specimens that way for sale. The doctor was at least once investigated by the local militia, perhaps following a tip off, but his servant and the local people always stood by him because he was also a generous man. He provided medical services to the poor, so taking the occasional liberty with a body that no one wanted could be perhaps be overlooked. Some paid him in kind and he is reputed to have also given away goods he didn't need for himself.

Another tale about this man, rather gruesome but of the period, tarts when a group of militia were called to visit over a man who'd been injured in a bar room fight, a stab wound to his midriff. His wife, a prostitute, had brought him to the doctor to treat the wound and then gone back to work. Later when she went back to get him she found him gone. She accused the doctor of killing him and the militia was sent for. They investigated but found nothing of the man. She told them what had happened and the doctor told them that he had left earlier. Knowing the militia of the area were unpaid men he offered them some recompense for their trouble. He opened his larder to them and on the slab was meat. It looked like pork and to men who didn't get meat very often it was a welcome gift. He told them to help themselves as some people paid him in goods not money. Whether it was pork (or 'long pig' as the Fijian's call it) we'll never know but around this time there was a law in Sheffield that butchers must always sell meat with the skin still in place so that it could be identified. Perhaps all kinds of strange meats were being sold at the time!

There have been other strange goings on at the building since its conversion. The penthouse on the building has a tale to tell too. The residents of the penthouse are at the moment a group of surgeons from the Northern General Hospital. They moved in as a group and took over the four-bedroom apartment, each person having a key to their own room. One afternoon one of the residents got home after a shift at 3 p.m. and after doing a quick cleaning job on the bathroom sat down with a cup of coffee and the paper. Unfortunately when he went to the fridge he found that his flatmates had used all the milk. He went out to get some more and was away for no more than five minutes. When he returned he heard the sound of water running in the bathroom and called out to his supposed flatmate but getting no reply he looked inside. The taps were on full, as was the shower, the bath was full to the brim, as was the sink, and the bath takes a full ten minutes to fill. Shutting off the water and mopping up with the towels he made everything good again and looked for his absent minded flatmate. He was alone, entirely alone; the rest of his colleagues came home around 7 p.m. and he was pale when they got there. He recounted his tale to them and they just laughed it off at first, until one of them opened his room to find that someone had been through his personal surgical equipment and replaced them wrongly, as if they'd been studied and looked at, then carefully replaced in their holders. Nothing else had been disturbed and the room has only one key. The ghost of the Penny Doctor seems to have moved up to the penthouse. Does he enjoy listening to their conversations about work, about the new techniques they use and possibly their accounts of those that never made it out of *their* operating theatre?

One of the doctors, a female surgeon, has actually moved out of the penthouse now because she feels that the ghost is 'watching' her constantly.

We often find that 'sensitive people' and mediums join our city tours and nowadays we ask before we pass this part of the tour in case they need warning of its history. On several tours such people have been disturbed by it, feeling sick or 'sweaty', and on one occasion two mediums (who didn't introduce themselves initially) had seen the door of the building 'flooded with blood that ran uphill' toward Campo Lane. Both had to leave the tour to recover their nerves and stomachs after being near the building and they went home soon after!

The Star Newspaper Offices (York Street)

This building looks too young to have any old or ghostly associations within its modern heart but the ground underneath it is another matter entirely. The *Star* offices have a room underneath the main printing floor that was used to put the typeface into blocks before the modern printing sheets used today. The room itself is no longer used, even to store goods, as the reputation of the room is enough to ensure that no one approaches it and rarely even mentions it anymore.

The room has seen a variety of unexplained incidents: notable among these are fights between friends, arguments over small things that escalated into violence and typeface that was set in its bed ready for the press but would be wrong and covered in blasphemy and swearing when it came to be used. The room was finally closed after one typesetter almost killed his friend with a bottle, having had no idea what he was doing until he was pulled off his friend and brought out of the room.

What the force is that's under this building no one really knows, but research puts the old spring well that served Hartshead directly under it. The well is marked on maps dating back to the early 1700s and many old artefacts were found in it, including broken combs, silver brooches, pins and earrings suggesting that the well had some significance to local people other than as a source of drinking and bathing water.

The Saxon Cross found near the cathedral was once next to the well. It's no surprise that the Wild Hunt is supposed to run out from Hartshead and down Campo Lane, out of the old sacred well and into the city. Who knows what type of ghoulish creature might lurk down in the old print room?

The old typesetting rooms that built the text that made The Iris, *then* The Star *and* Sheffield Telegraph. *It was in a typesetting room like this in the basement that a strange entity made itself felt.*

It's a fact that the workers who've been there for a while soon learn of its reputation and even those in the buildings around it know of the cellar room. A building that abuts the back of the old *Telegraph* building and shares an alleyway with it was to have its telephone lines replaced in the early 1990s. When the engineers from British Telecom arrived they took one look at the building and refused to go into the cellars, as 'There's been trouble here before'. The wires were brought in

Fargate and Telegraph *building. An old graveyard was exposed here when the new tram tracks were being put in.*

at ground level. Even the workmen who serviced the buildings knew about the reputation of the room under the *Star* building, avoiding it if they can. Those who have worked with the building have reported a variety of incidents over the years: slaps and taps felt, voices speaking their names in their ears as they work. Even a ghostly tape measure has been felt and a voice enquiring of a young gentleman, 'Excuse me sir but what side does one dress upon?' This quote leads us neatly into the story of a second ghost of the *Star* building who appears to have moved from his old premises across York Street to the new offices when the modern workforce went over.

The ghost is a tailor and we believe it to be a Mr Wilfred Lyons, who used to own a 'Saville Row' tailors on the same premises. The ghost's favourite trick is to come up behind someone while they're working and try to take their measurements, even going so far as to ask women what bust size they are.

One such incident occurred when he was still haunting the old offices on York Street in the early 1970s. A woman wearing a mini-skirt was typing at a desk in the reception. She was working quite happily until suddenly she shot back from her desk red faced and looked under her desk. When asked what the matter was she explained that someone had just 'touched her with something cold at the top of her thighs'. The tailor no doubt was looking for another customer. He's even been felt on the printing floor today with men turning to each other wondering why they want to know 'what side of the bed they get dressed on'. He's still active in the offices today and I've seen his work for myself in the building – still looking for new fashions and new hemlines.

Another ghost is of a little girl who still haunts the old offices of the *Star* on York Street. Before the new building was erected this whole area used to be the lawyers' quarter of Sheffield. The ghost is thought to be the youngest daughter of the family who once lived here. Being a lawyer sometimes draws criminals to take revenge. One night a gang who'd lost their leader to the hangman's noose at the Leeds Assizes because of this particular lawyer decided that they'd send a message to the rest of the lawyers of Sheffield. Breaking into the house they rounded up the sleeping family and proceeded to kill and torture them, keeping the youngest girl alive as a testament to their work and what would happen if anyone else tried to hurt them. Sadly, though she too died from the brutal attack and now haunts the house where she lived and died.

Her ghost is said to hate its reflection and has been blamed for the smashing of two floor-to-ceiling mirrors that used to be behind the front desk of the *Star* newspaper. Her voice was heard giggling as she did it, running away to hide on the stairs, which are now boarded in by dark glass that, gives no true reflection. Her hands are still felt by customers in the old *Star* offices. She reaches out to young men mostly as if she's trying to get help, tugging on jackets and trousers for attention. One evening on a tour through the area a group of people saw the shadowy figure of a little girl running across the carpeted floor and hiding behind a desk. They described her as blonde, with no face to speak of but her dress is cut up and dirty in places. She's a lonely little ghost, lost in the building that was built over her old home, still searching for the help that never came when she was alive.

Cavendish Court (Bank Street)

Cavendish Court is now a Job Centre and Benefits Office but it has seen a variety of uses over the years. In recent memory it has been a nightclub (several different names), a cabaret club and a public house in the early 1930s. Before this is was a private house but it's the public house period that's of interest to us now. The ghost is of a little man who is believed to have died in the pub which was known as the George and Dragon. The man is between forty and forty-five years of age, dressed in a tweed suit with a flat cap, small rounded glasses and he has a Sheffield accent. He asks the same question to every person he appears to and he did this to me personally when we first went to Cavendish Court; he asks, 'Excuse me, could you please direct me to the shop with the three bulls-eye panes of glass in the window?' He waits for your answer and if you don't know it he disappears when your back's turned. I had been greeted by the old man with this question. I didn't know the answer so we began to walk away from him when it occurred to me that there was a small shop up Figtree Lane that had bulls-eye glass and I turned back to ask him if it was there but he had vanished. There was no sign of him at all on the street and we had only been just a few steps away from him.

When we related this tale to members of one of our tours, one man exclaimed loudly, 'Thank God I'm not the only one he's done this to!' The man in question had been approached by the same man and been asked precisely the same question when passing the building. He too had turned around to ask him if it was the shop on Figtree lane but found the little man had disappeared.

This man isn't only found on the street, he's also been seen inside the new building holding a half pint of beer and looking rather sad. When approached by the security staff he just winks out. In fact, an ex-barman of the Corporation Nightclub who used to own the premises before the building was converted into offices used to send new staff to get him out of the premises, only to see him wink out when they reached out toward him, causing several new staff to leave after only a few nights.

There is also a female ghost residing here. She has been seen dressed in a royal purple Victorian-style dress with a bustle. She was seen when the club was called Romeo and Juliet's in 1970 when Sir Norman Wisdom was playing there. A councillor and his wife were entertaining friends at the club when he noticed the woman dressed in all her finery walking through the packed club. He nudged his wife who also saw her moving through the crowds and commented on her beautiful dress, wondering if she was part of the act to come. They both witnessed her walk right through several people before finally fading out all together. They were left in no doubt about what they had seen.

This ghost is still around but nowadays she's little more than a drifting cloud of Gardenia perfume, often noticed in the area of the ladies toilets in the building at the back of the offices. A cold spot that never warms is also reported to exist there too. People employed in other businesses around the back of the building (which backs onto a large loading bay) have smelt her perfume and felt her presence. It has been suggested that she was the wife of James the coachman who lived at the Brown Bear public house. She was set up as a mistress to a wealthy man on Bank street in an apartment. But how she met her end we can only guess.

The Boardwalk (Bank Street)

The Boardwalk has been a live music venue for over thirty years and has gone by many different names over this time, including The Black Swan and The Mucky Duck, but it's the music that gets the most attention now and not the ghost.

The ghost has made itself felt along the corridor that leads to the stage from the backstage are. Several people have felt someone brush by them as they walk down the narrow corridor but have seen no one. One man had his arm grabbed by someone just before he stepped out on stage. People have held séances to try to contact the departed that are seemingly gathering at The Boardwalk. One séance held recently saw a group of staff having a go, just 'for a laugh', and ending with everyone frightened as the glass revolved faster and faster until it fell over.

On one occasion a band had to abandon its set on stage because a guitar lead would not stay put in the amplifier socket. Repeatedly the guitarist replaced the offending plug, even finally taping it in place, but each time it came free. There was no obvious explanation for this except that someone unseen was having some fun pulling it out. Whoever they were the ghost didn't like the sound of them and they cut short their set on stage, leaving with the ghost's approval. It has also been said that there's an old groupie waiting in the Boardwalk, dressed in leopard print, who waits for young musicians to pass by and then she pinches their bottoms or strokes them as they pass her by. Her presence has even been noticed in the toilets as well; it's been said if she's found someone she likes she'll follow him around until closing time.

The Fountain Public House (Leopold Street)

The Fountain Public House occupies a spot that was home to a makeshift hospital and mortuary during the Second World War. The present building was built in 1976 covering the older land plot and taking on apparently the ghosts that still haunt this area. It has been reported that the cellars of the public house are somewhere never to go to alone: several bar staff have been accosted by ghosts in the depths of the dark cellar. Staff have been touched, pinched and grabbed on the legs by invisible hands, as if the dying who were brought there after the Sheffield Blitz were still trying to get help from the hospital staff. The pub staff do their work down there in pairs, and with the lights on, hoping the unquiet dead don't decide to rise up and join them in the bar upstairs too which, fortunately, they haven't yet done.

St James Chapel (St James Place)

St James's chapel was built in 1778 as a relief chapel for Glebe Street and the surrounding area. The chapel could hold 700 people in its iron column supported majesty. The chapel had a graveyard attached to it but it also had a crypt beneath it for the great and the good to be buried in while they awaited the clarion call. Sadly, the peaceful slumbers of the dead in the crypt were disturbed when the chapel took a direct hit during the air raid of 12 December 1940. Most of the building collapsed in on itself but the crypt survived underneath with only a hole in the marble floor covering it. It was through this new entrance that two thieves entered the crypt in search of valuables to steal from the dead. Little did they know what was in store for them!

The men entered the crypt the night after the Blitz, hoping to find something of value, perhaps to strip the coffins of their fittings or to find something of greater worth inside them. They split up and went to opposite ends of the crypt hoping to find enough in the darkness to make the risk worthwhile. One man went to the back of the crypt and finding a large sarcophagus he opened it up to find a Victorian lady inside. He stripped off the necklace and brooch but struggled with her rings so finally decided to take her thin dry fingers with the rings still attached. He moved off to the next coffin with his gruesome gains and gave his partner a quick glance to see if he was still alright. What he saw made him stop dead in his tracks.

His partner had just lifted a pocket watch and hip flask from an Edwardian gentleman lying in his coffin but what he hadn't noticed was the creature climbing up his leg from the floor! His first thought was that this could be someone who was injured in the bombing and got trapped in the crypt. When he shone his light on the scene they both saw that this was no living creature but a corpse-like thing with matted hair and long fingernails. It began to howl as it clung to his partner's leg. That was quite enough for him and he ran hell for leather toward the collapsed part of the crypt and the way out. Pushing past his partner he caught full sight of the creature and heard its piercing scream as he flew past. Leaving his friend behind to fend for himself with the terrible apparition he came face to face with two sets of feet, booted feet, as he climbed out...

Looking up he met the gaze of two policemen who were doing the rounds of the bombed buildings looking for looters. In a state of severe shock he let them help him out of the hole and they kept him next to the building. All the while the sound of screaming could be heard in the crypt alerting the two policemen to the presence of someone else inside. They were about to go inside themselves when his injured friend appeared at the hole. The policemen grabbed him and helped him out too and sat him at the kerbside. Asked what they'd been doing down there, both men confessed and emptied their pockets to show the spoils of the night. Before they took them to the station the older of the two policemen told the younger to investigate while he kept an eye on the two men. The young policeman went into the crypt but found nothing amiss except the opened coffins so he reported back to his superior and they accompanied the thieves to the station for questioning.

The men were seen first by a police physician, one requiring stitches to cuts on his chest and face, before being questioned. The injured man seemed more lucid than his partner, who seemed to be in deep shock. He related their tale, 'We were in the crypt trying to find what we could to steal when I felt this 'thing' on my leg, climbing up me slowly, its mouth open and screaming. I tried to get it off but it just clung on and tried to kill me. I punched at it but it was too fast and I ended up on the floor with it. It slashed at me with its claws but I kicked it away, ran to the exit and scrambled out.' His friend meanwhile was rocking back and forth, lost in the horror of what he'd seen, and repeating, 'My God, my God we've opened the gates to hell'. This man was sent to a psychiatric hospital for treatment and beyond that we know nothing of his fate.

Above and opposite: St James chapel was destroyed in the Blitz of 1940 but a pair of looters got more than they bargained for when they entered the ruined crypt.

As for his accomplice, no charges were made against him; he gave back the things he'd stolen and it seems no one really wanted to send him up to the judge after what had happened. He reputedly went back to work in the steelworks the next day with only a caution; probably the police thought he'd suffered punishment enough already. Over the next few months his hair turned white and his tale became part of the modern folklore of Sheffield.

On the site of the old chapel and its crypt in St James Place is now an office block and in 2005 security guards from the building saw a strange apparition staggering across the car park. Thinking at first it was probably a drunk needing assistance one guard went out to investigate only to find that it wasn't what he thought it was. Instead he watched an awful apparition in rags shuffle over the car park and fade out where the old graveyard used to be. The only other thing he heard was a high-pitched wail like a siren on the breeze. Disturbed he went back inside and checked the camera's and yes the apparition was there when he checked it but the next morning the tape was blank.

The creature that haunted the crypt could be a sort of banshee, a guardian of the dead, although banshees are usually associated with the Irish and their folklore. Perhaps there was an Irish family buried in the crypt protected by its own personal banshee! A woman's scream has often been heard in the area over the years but there is housing close by it's possible it comes from there, yet the keening wail that is heard is quite distinct and high pitched and on many a winter's night it has been heard near the car park. Now when the security guards hear it they keep their eyes glued to the CCTV screen and hope that they'll not see the shambling figure crossing the car park again.

St James Place today.

The Museum Public House (Orchard Square)

There have been reports of hauntings in this building since the late 1800s. The building has been a private house and a mortuary and was converted into a public house at a later date. The ghost is thought to be a someone who was a brought to the mortuary when he wasn't dead or was perhaps suffering from catalepsy. But whoever the ghost is his focus of interest seems to be the beer that the pub provides and has a great dislike for beer with bubbles in it! When the public house went onto artificially-gassed beers in the late 1950s troubles with the ghost began. He first started moving things around in the cellar and generally being a nuisance to those running the cellars. His activities escalated as more bottles were delivered and more pumps turned from traditional-style ale to the new modern gassed beers and lagers.

One landlord in particular who had a rough time with him was Mr Ernest Bray. He would get deliveries of gas and beer, set things up in the cellar and then find that as he went to pull

The Museum Public House where a ghost prefers to drink Real Ale and used to pour beer over the customers.

a fresh pint, the beer would arrive flat from the pump. Putting it down to old beer still in the lines he'd pull another, only to have this come up flat too. He'd go down into the cellar again and find the gas line had been disconnected and the lock disengaged. Puzzled, he'd hook the gas back up to the pumps and return to pull another pint. This might work for a while but as the bar became busy and there was a crowd waiting to be served then the gas would stop again and flat beer would be drawn. Going back into the cellar Ernest would find the line had been disconnected again. This was not all, because often he'd also find that bottles were missing, later to be found hidden behind the empty barrels awaiting pick-up from the brewery. So as well as reconnecting the gas he'd have to manhandle the bottles back into position for use before he could continue to serve upstairs.

The trouble didn't limit itself to the cellar though, as the ghost seems to have had certain ideas about who should be in the pub and who shouldn't. Often it was attractive young women who bore the brunt of his attentions. He would cause beer glasses to be knocked over near them or pull chairs roughly out from beneath them as they went to sit down, as if he was trying to drive them out of the pub. Once he even took someone's beer order and poured it directly down the sink, in full view of the customers and the bar staff. Was this to show his displeasure at their choice of drink?

He did calm down his antics after the pub changed back to a Real Ale public house again, serving real ale alongside modern bottled beers. It appears though that he may have turned his attention later to a new, shiny acquisition that the pub installed. Like a lot of modern pubs The Museum opened a small coffee bar in the front of the pub on the Orchard Square side. It seems that the old ghost is a bit of a traditionalist and took offence to the modern coffee machine making Italian coffee! The ghost would play with the steam generator, making it build pressure to a dangerous level: maybe he was hoping to have it explode and destroy the machine so it couldn't be used again. Eventually they replaced the machine with one that has a safety release valve that opens when the pressure builds too high and this foils his dangerous tricks.

The ghost still makes his feelings felt here occasionally but he has been much quieter of late, seeing as he now has a pub where he can drink real ale. The present landlord doesn't have the same problems as Ernest did but we reckon it's only a matter of time before the old ghost works out that the gassed beer he hated so much is sold in bottles behind the bar. Until then, if you visit the pub, I recommend you should play it safe and buy the local ale, he's less likely to spill it.

THREE

EXCHANGE STREET TO PONDS FORGE

EXCHANGE STREET TO PONDS FORGE

Castle Square (old Hole in the Road)

Now this is something that not many people may realise but the Old Hole in the Road (where Fitzalan Square tram stop is today) used to have a GT News shop underneath the Bankers Draft. The ghost that haunts here was a useful one; she would clean up the back room of the newsagents, leaving a pile of dirt to be swept up in the morning by the first person to come in. But it was her method of communication that set her out from so many others. Leading into the old basements was a telephone wire that used to run to an old-fashioned black phone. One day it was brought out of the cellar and left on the shelf next to the cash register as a talking piece for the customers. The wire was disconnected as far as everyone knew and it surprised them one day by ringing at the end of a day's trade!

Picking up the phone the assistant heard a woman's voice on the other end of it talking in a broad Sheffield accent. She wasn't waiting to be answered – she just kept on telling them what she was doing and what her life was like. Thinking they had a crossed line they put the phone down but the thing happened again the next week and they decided to check the line out. They were told that the phone line was definitely disconnected and as such it couldn't be ringing let alone have someone speaking on the other end of it.

The calls to this phone and the woman's voice carried on until the closure of the Hole in the Road in the early part of the 1990s, although her last call did at least let them see who they'd been listening to after all the years of contact. When the shop was closing down they had four spinner card racks in the front window displaying what they had left to sell. When they were shutting up in the last week of trading they had moved the card racks from the window, and what they saw was an old char woman sitting with a pot of tea along with a tin mug at a card table. She just smiled at them both and then faded away, as if she knew it was time to stop work now and give up the ghost.

The strange sequel to this is that she might just still be trying to communicate by phone! The Hole in the Road may have been filled in but the spirit of the old char lady could now be using the first phone box just up from the tram stop. How do I know? My wife has answered the phone when passing and heard it ringing; the sound she says was like a crossed wire, scratchy and old with echoes in it. The woman on the other end just kept talking about work and what she was doing in a broad Sheffield accent.

Castle Square where the 'Telephone Ghost' made herself known.

Maybe she was a woman who cleaned the building next to Cochran's nearby; both buildings were destroyed during the Blitz on 12 December 1940. Taking shelter under the building in the cellars she was killed while waiting to phone someone and tell them she was safe and not to worry.

The Market Tavern (Exchange Street)

This tavern was built in 1849 and was always popular place to come to. The pub was a Berni Inn from 1969 to 1984 and had a restaurant in the lower floor of the inn called the Garden Restaurant but to the regulars and the people living around it had always been called 'The Old Number Twelve'.

The inn itself had a stage and performers often played there to packed houses, but the ghost who lives in the Tavern today is an ex-miner called Charlie. When children were still used to work in the mines Charlie had finished his shift and was at The Old Number Twelve having a drink when news came that there had been a 'cave in' at the mine and a child was trapped. Charlie went back and offered to help free the trapped child but unfortunately lost his own life in the process.

His ghost was often seen afterwards in the old downstairs bar, his shadowy shape seen sitting next to someone as they took a quiet drink after work. He was also heard to sigh heavily and was heard by many customers to do so. He was often heard sighing by women too as if he'd been looking at them and realising he could no longer touch them.

When the Berni Inn was remodelled to a more modern style Charlie was seen in the cellars where he would often open the door to the cellars and look out to see if things had gone back to normal before pulling his head back into the cellar. Glasses were seen to move on their own across the lower bar as if Charlie was trying to get a drink down to him. As the upper part of the pub changed Charlie kept himself more and more to the cellar. As the years wore on the pub began to lose its clientele and it is now a derelict building, shuttered up awaiting redevelopment. Just before it closed the pub company put back most of the original features that had been taken out when Berni Inns had first owned it, recapturing some of the Victorian glory it had once had. We can only hope that whoever redevelops the building will keep Charlie in mind when they finally get started.

Ponds Forge Tram Stop

This area is a little bit of an oddity so this is why its included here; the tram stops basically follow the older routes that used to run from the town centre and Ponds Forge is one such stop. Yet the strangeness that afflicts this stop hasn't just been felt in modern times, it even happened when the trams first began running.

People would just step off the platform in front of the trams, not realising what they were doing or why. Several pedestrians were killed in this way and people were at a loss to know why. When the new trams were introduced they used the old plans and decided to reopen the old tram stop at Ponds Forge and as they did so the accidents started up again. Several people have just stepped out in front of moving trams, as if in a trance, not realising what they were doing or why. When they come round and wonder what all the fuss is about they're genuinely shocked to find that they had apparently been trying to commit suicide. I've seen this happen myself three times in the ten years of the trams running again in Sheffield.

This stop is close to a road crossing that has taken more than its fair share of deaths. The crossing lights that accompany the tram stop are opposite Cooplands bakery and the staff at the shop have been witnesses to many gruesome accidents at the crossing. One woman who was waiting to cross said 'It was as if he didn't even care, he just stepped out in front of the bus and it hit him square on.'

The ghost that haunts here is a young man who appears on the tram side of the crossing in the early hours. He waits for someone to cross with, then he tries to push them into traffic. One lady was coming back from a nightshift and as she stood waiting with what she thought was another night worker the young man barged into her and almost pushed her under a truck

Tram tracks leading to Ponds Forge. The crossing in front of Ponds Forge has always been an accident black spot.

that was passing through the lights. She turned angrily to speak to the young man but he was nowhere to be seen, she was alone on the crossing. She went home and told her family about the incident and her husband told her that he had heard tales about the crossing from bus drivers. They like to avoid the routes its on because of its reputation for accidents. Even when the road was just a coaching route people died in accidents that seemed to stem from the river basin below the crossing points.

The Marples Hotel (Fitzalan Square)

As we have seen Sheffield suffered badly in the Blitz and the night of 12 December 1940 saw many tragedies. The Marples Hotel used to sit at the corner of Fitzalan Square and during the

The Marples Hotel was rebuilt over the rubble of the earlier one destroyed in the Blitz. Over seventy souls died there in 1940 and the sickly sweet smell of death still haunts the building.

war was a residence for billeted soldiers. But what made the bombing of the hotel particularly bad was that at the time of the raid a winter dance was being held at the hotel. The entire place was packed with guests as well as staff. The hotel took a direct hit and the only things standing were the side windows of the hotel and the pile of rubble that had been the roof and walls of the building. Only seven people survived that night; the rest were lost in the destruction of the building but there are several very strange tales linked with this night of destruction.

One is of a tram guard who was in his tram when the attack came. His tram was blown over and he was seen clambering out of the wreckage after seeing to his own passengers and running up the road toward the next stop (Cricket Inn Road) to warn the next tram. The tram driver saw him and stopped his tram and the passengers inside all hid beside the tracks until the raid was over. He'd saved nearly seventy lives on both trams and took a seat at the back of the tram after the raid was over and rode it back into the city centre. When it came for the accounts to be taken down by the tram bosses at the scene they asked for the tram guard who'd run all the way up the hill after saving his own passengers. They found him eventually, lying under his own tram; the blast had killed him outright but seventy people had seen him and taken his help after his death.

We stay with the trams for this next story of a young woman who was a tram guard and who'd just finished her shift at eleven. She'd left her white gloves behind on the tram and was going to go back and get them when a voice rang through her house telling her to get into the cellar. She was frightened and so she did it; the next morning she woke to find her name listed with seventy others believed killed in the bombing of the Marples Hotel. The next tram guard had handed her gloves into the hotel's doorman, who she knew well. He died and her gloves were found nearby with her name written inside them. When she went into work that day she worked out that if she'd left when she'd planned to she'd have been at the doors of the hotel when the bomb dropped. The voice saved her life and, as she learned later, the doorman's life too: he'd been asked by the day man if he could swap shifts with him as he wanted to work the party for tips later. He'd agreed: it had been the day-shift doorman who'd died in the bombing and not her friend.

Now we move onto Marples itself. When the air-raid sirens went off most of the partygoers went into the cellars, thinking that the ceiling would support the blast if they got hit. Unfortunately they took a direct hit and the rubble collapsed into the cellars killing almost everyone there immediately, the others who were left identifiable were killed by the fumes of alcohol boiling. The carbon dioxide filled the room slowly and gassed the remaining survivors. The smell when they finally got to the bottom of the cellars was 'sickly sweet', like a room filled with flowers. Not all the bodies could be removed from the old place and not everyone who was lost was accounted for in the wreckage. But Marples was rebuilt in the late 1950s and the ghost that's attached to the building isn't a person or an act, it's a smell. Sometimes it's something like pork cooking, others like a florists filled with honeysuckle. The smell has been reported more than once to me on the Steel City Ghost Tour by people who assume it's the flats above the new Hein Geriecke store. But the windows can't be opened to send smells out of the flats above; what people are experiencing is the scent of bodies burning and the smell of burning alcohol as it filtered through the rubble. Today a Ladbrokes Turf Accountants use the cellars of the old Marples building but we've yet to come across any ghost stories from the ladies who work there.

The Victorian Post Office (Flat Street)

This grand old building was built in 1897 but its old workers and residents still come and use the building even though it's due for development in late 2006; the old brick part of this magnificent structure was once used as the Postman's Social Club where men, and eventually women, could be found playing darts, cards or snooker on the tables after work. Because of the unsocial hours the workers had to endure the social club was open nearly twenty-four hours a day but now the building is all closed and empty – or so we thought. There have been numerous reports of activity in the building since it was vacated and these have most often been noticed on Sunday evenings between the hours of eleven and twelve.

What's heard coming from the now empty building is the sound of laughter and the sound of snooker balls running over the tables, people having a good time and unwinding after work. I have even seen evidence of this myself. One night on my way home from a trip to Doncaster I passed the building and noticed the lights were shining onto the road and I heard the sounds of

Above and opposite: *The Victorian Post Office where old postmen, it seems, never die.*

fun coming from the building itself. I decided to ask a friend who had worked in the building if the social club was being used again as we believed it had been closed since the 1980s. He confirmed that the building had indeed been closed for years and also that others too had reported seeing lights and hearing sounds from this part of the building. There had also been tales from postmen still working in the building, as the move was gradually being made to new premises at Meadowhall, of strange happenings. Several times people had seen mail move on its own across the sorting tables, even turning up in the wrong pigeon-holes and needing to be sorted again. When this mail was examined it was noticed that it was sometimes being sorted to the old layout of the office, as if some 'old workers' were trying to help out the staff of the day but not knowing of the current layout.

These buildings are due to become a hotel and shopping arcade in the next year or so and, knowing how some of the ghosts of Sheffield like to stay around, we might expect to hear that some of these are trying to help the new staff and businesses: after all, the city does have a reputation for having workers who never want to go home.

The Old Queens Head today.

The Old Queens Head (Pond Street)

The Old Queens Head building was originally constructed in the 1400s as a marsh hunting lodge and was listed by the Earl of Shrewsbury in his inventory of properties in 1582. The building has undergone many changes and renovations over its time, the most recent being in the early 1990s when the pub became part of the Tom Cobleigh company chain.

There are ghosts active in this building as the landlady who runs the pub will attest to. One ghost limits itself to activities in the ladies lavatories on the ground floor! The lavatory occupies space that was once part of the road that ran in front of the Old Queens Head which led to the water marshes and a wash-house that was next to the original hall. Perhaps the ghost still uses the road, unaware of the disturbances he or she is causing to the comfort of the pub's female clientele.

The Old Queens Head has seen many ghosts over the years.

A typical experience is reported here : 'I was sitting in the far right cubicle, totally alone in the ladies, no one was above in the private room so the noises I heard couldn't have come from anywhere else but the room I was in. I had just sat down when the lock on the door began to open, I watched the bar lock turn to open and had the presence of mind to put my foot against the bottom of the door and said, 'Occupied'. Locking the door again I listened for sounds of anyone else in the toilets with me but there was not a sound. I hadn't heard the main door open and couldn't hear anything, not even breathing. Then the door lock began to open again, I became quite disturbed and called out again ,'Occupied' and kept my foot at the bottom of the door and re-locked it for a second time. The 'presence' then appeared to have moved away from my cubicle and entered the one to my right because I heard the toilet roll dispenser moving as if someone was pulling out paper. Curious, I listened for a while and the pulling stopped after a few moments. On leaving I took a look into the empty cubicle next to mine but apart from a few sheets of paper on the floor there was no sign that anyone had been there and I had not heard anyone leaving.'

The ghost that frequents the toilets may be the same ghost that caused some trouble to an ex-landlady and her staff, a washer-woman, who had been employed to collect all the dirty washing from the hall and return it after it had been cleaned. Lisa (the landlady who owned the pub from 1990-93) used to find her uniform going missing regularly but it would always return after a day or so but it would smell freshly washed but she could never distinguish what powder or liquid it had been washed in.

This wasn't the only ghostly visitation that she had to put up with. Her deputy manager Susan had a Rottweiler called Aiesha that she'd bring to work with her and leave upstairs in the rooms. Aiesha was a friendly bitch and often gave customers a lick or greeted them at the bar when she was downstairs. This began to change after she had been left upstairs one evening. There was a large party in the bar and the dog was locked upstairs in the main room with the television on for company. Around 10 o'clock she started howling and didn't stop but as the bar was busy no one came to see to her until after it had closed. When someone went upstairs to see what was causing her such distress they found her locked outside the room on a small balcony. The French windows to the room were locked on the inside. When they let her back inside she continued to growl and took great interest in one corner of the room. Aiesha obviously didn't like being in the room anymore and chose to go downstairs and wait for her mistress there. There was no way Aiesha could have opened the French doors herself and then locked them again from the other side.

On another occasion when Aiesha was upstairs in the same room above the bar they heard an almighty crash. Everyone rushed upstairs to find Aiesha again on the balcony, apparently having been thrown through the French doors! Her fur was bloody and she was shaking with fear. After a visit to the vet the consensus view was that Aiesha had done it herself, perhaps trying to chase after a bus she'd seen through the windows. The trouble with this idea was that the dog never chased after vehicles and had a quiet disposition. Jumping through a window was not in keeping with this animal at all. After this incident Aiesha was given away and when she came to visit her ex-mistress she refused to enter the pub. She'd sit down at the front door but she never entered the building again and become aggressive if anyone tried to force her inside. Was it a ghost that caused this dog to be so frightened that it tried to escape through a glass door?

The Old Queens Head has been remodelled more than once over the years and each time the work seems to arouse a different apparition to revisit an old stamping ground. When the front of the bar that faces the street (the oldest part of the building) was redone it caused one old visitor to return; a Civil War soldier. We know that Oliver Cromwell ordered Sheffield castle to be taken and the forces there to be disbanded; the Earl of Manchester tried to take the castle but it was the Duke of Arundel (John Bright, after whom Brightside is named) who succeeded. He brought heavy cannon and pounded the castle, breaking their resistance after an eight-day siege. The castle was finally destroyed in August 1644. The ghost at the Old Queens Head is thought to be one of John Bright's men, a Puritan solider, but he's only been seen in the old main hall, next to the original fireplace that dates back to the first use of the building in the fifteenth century. He has been seen reflected in the bottom breastplate of four hung on the fireplace. He stands in full uniform holding two large flagons of ale or wine, looking around the room as if he recognises the place but not the furnishings or people. He has been seen by several people as they've been eating in what has now become a dining room for the pub. All the reports are from afternoon sightings, he has not been seen at any other time.

Another ghost at the pub is one that has been seen there over many years and is still appearing today. The ghost is of a little old man who used to be a pub regular and used to sit in what was the snug area of the bar. He has been observed on and off since the 1970s. When the remodelling of this part of the pub went ahead the snug wall was removed to create an open bar area that now wraps around the entire pub. He has appeared to the cleaners in the morning, holding a half pint of beer in his hand, and then gently fades away as they came into the room to clean. One cleaner called Audrey would often shout, 'Good Morning!' into the snug, before entering to give the ghost chance to fade away before she went inside. Recently an investigation was done by a local paranormal group into the ghosts of the Old Queens Head and this gentleman was picked up by their medium. He sits in the snug and quietly drinks his beer when everyone else has gone home. When the old snug was still separated off he would often reopen the door between the snug and the main bar, opening the bolts and switching on the pumps, so he could get himself a beer after hours.

The refurbished pub also seems to suffer from the old man's desire to clear out the pub early. His main trick is to make the snug lights flicker and dwindle at the old chucking out time of 11.15 p.m. People look at the lights and check their watches, wondering if the bar staff are dipping the lights to remind people it's time to drink up. I've often been there when this has occurred. Apparently the lights were all redone when the refurbishments were done in the mid-1990s and they've had the lights checked and they can't find any fault with the new wiring or the lights. I think the old man wants the people to leave so he can have his drink and relax in his favourite spot in the snug without anyone interfering. Not a bad idea of paradise for some people.

Now this next ghost may not even seem like one but it certainly put the wind up the landlord at the time; a phantom pint of beer. The landlord was Mr Butler who when cleaning up with his staff at the end of the evening found, on many occasions, a full pint of beer abandoned on a small table in the snug. He began to get irate about this pint and questioned the staff to see if any of them remembered serving it or had noticed who might be leaving it there. None of the staff knew anything about the pint and one night while cleaning up Mr Butler tasted it and found to his amazement that he didn't recognise the beer at all; it wasn't one served by the pub! Deciding he would get to the bottom of the mystery he told his staff to leave the pint in place next time it turned up and to leave the table unwiped for the night as well.

So the pint was left on the table the next night until the following morning. When Mr Butler came down he found his snug door unbolted and the pumps turned on and the pint glass was empty and the dregs were still running down the inside of the glass. He looked closely at the glass and the dust on the table for fingerprints but found none, only the recently emptied glass. As he set up for the rest of the day he decided that at the end of the night he'd set up his video camera and film the snug that night. There was only one problem for this plan; when he came to clear up for the night the pint wasn't there and it hasn't been seen since. Whoever was waiting for the pint got it eventually, after patiently waiting for it to be left overnight, but who could it have been?

Finally, at the Old Queens Head, we move from a haunted pint to a piece of haunted furniture. An old cabinet believed to have been in the house since its earliest days was kept in one of the living rooms upstairs in the pub in the 1990s when the pub manager was Susan. Her barmaid Nicola had the piece of furniture in her room but it was too big and took up too much space, so she asked for it to be put in the cellar. It took several men a few hours to get it downstairs into the cellar but it went in eventually. Nicloa used to do the changeovers of the barrels in the cellar when they ran dry and she often went down to get more bottles and such. One night she went down to change over the barrels and she got the shock of her life! She heard a noise and looked round to find the old cabinet was moving toward her on its small wooden feet. The heavy old thing crept across the cellar toward her as she stood there in shock. Finally she managed to break spell and ran up the stairs to the bar and told the staff what had happened. They came down with her and saw the cabinet well away from the wall where it had been and halfway toward the stairs. It was as if the cabinet wanted to go back upstairs where it belonged instead of in the cold dark cellar! As far as we know the piece was never taken back upstairs and may still be down in the cellar bemoaning its lot in its old age.

FOUR

THE DON AND AROUND

THE DON AND AROUND

The Old Crown Inn (Scotland Street)

The tale of this ghost is one that plucks the heartstrings of even the hardest heart. The ghost is of a worker who came back to work after an untimely death. The man was a gentle giant who worked for the landlord in the early twentieth century looking after the cellars and beer barrels. His job was to work as long as the bar was open, which could be all hours because the pub served a few steelworks and factories. At this time there were no licensing laws for pubs and hotels so workers could find themselves working very long hours indeed. This landlord was more concerned about his profits than the health of his staff.

Often this landlord would beat his staff if they were slow in getting barrels changed or bringing up new crates of beer. He carried a stick ready for the purpose. One day the landlord called down to have a barrel changed and, receiving no reply, went down into the cellar and found his cellar man curled up on a pile of sacking and apparently sleeping on the job. Taking his stick he began to beat the man, only stopping when there was no sound or movement following the blows. Taking a closer look he realised the man was ill or dead. Running upstairs he called his wife to get the doctor who lived in the hotel to come down into the cellar. The doctor pronounced him dead of a heart attack and said that the beating had been given post-mortem. The landlord had escaped the hangman's noose for the murder he at first thought he had committed.

After the landlord died the ghost of the cellar man could often be heard working in the cellar, moving crates and sorting out the cellar. Even today he still 'helps out' and can be heard down in the cellar, especially if the bar upstairs is busy.

The Three Tuns (Silver Street Head)

There has been a public house on this site since at least 1745 but originally the Convent of St Vincent stood here stretching out over the area and across the road up Scotland Street. The ghost that haunts here is traditionally believed to be the ghost of a nun who died bricked up in the

The Old Crown Inn in Scotland Street where a cellar man's ghost can still be heard working among the barrels.

The Three Tuns pub today where history meets the present.

cellar of the old wash-house that stood on the ground where the pub does today. Exactly why she is thought to have been bricked up in the cellar we can only guess. The wash-house was next to Hick's field which was common grazing land at the time.

The present building was built in 1812 and during renovations a 'priest hole' was found in a wall as well as a secret room beneath the cellar. A body was also found at this time which was subsequently reburied at Sharrow cemetery and this point seems to have been the trigger for the hauntings that followed. The landlord at the time was the unfortunate Mr Conroy, who was also the landlord of the Brown Bear in our earlier story where he met the ghostly old coachman, James.

The ghostly nun can be heard in the cellar, moving things around and generally making a nuisance of herself. Once she so scared a landlord's elderly mother that she didn't want to stay and asked to be put into a care home! The ghost tends to limit herself mostly to the bar and the cellar areas although she has been felt upstairs, pinching and pulling at people on the stairs. The present landlord often hears the nun in the cellar when the door is left open and he also 'feels her presence' when he's down in the cellar, but doesn't see anything. She's not been touching or pinching him yet but she's been noticed by some of the older female customers who come into the pub. Women often speak of feeling 'watched' or 'uneasy' when they sit in the pointed end of the building, and shift around the pub until they find a comfortable spot. Female sobbing has often been heard in the cellars as if coming from behind a wall, soft and quiet but difficult to locate.

Queens Hotel (Scotland Street)

The Queens Hotel is just over the rise from The Old Crown Inn and was opened in 1797. It closed for the last time in 1997 having been known in its later years as a pub for extravagant parties and an open, 'anything goes' atmosphere.

Janet Bond was the licensee of the pub in 1989 when they found they had a musical ghost in their midst. The ghost played the pub's organ in the middle of the night, usually it seems around the midnight hour. The regular organist, who played the organ for the pub's customers, would complain the stops were left out and the pedals moved since he'd last played although no one had been near it. She told him that it was the ghost who was using the organ at night but not surprisingly, he didn't believe her. He eventually decided to stay after hours and wait with her to listen to the phantom organ player. They waited until nearly two in the morning but the ghost failed to appear so the organist left and went home. Soon after he'd gone the organ began to play again! It was as if the ghost didn't want to play in front of the man who had the daytime rights to it but when he had left he could play his own hour of music and leave again. Janet didn't try to get him removed even though he did caused her a few shocks during her tenancy. As far as she was concerned, he'd been there first and as such he should be left in peace.

Methodist Meeting Hall (Scotland Street)

The ghost that appears here has been seen on and off since the 1980s. She was first seen by a group of young YTS trainees doing their exams for the building trade. This ghost, a rather fierce looking nursing sister dressed in uniform, walked straight into the bay-windowed room that was being used as a classroom and began her ward rounds. The boys at the time thought someone had dressed up and was playing a joke on them until she walked through a desk! The room cleared and they refused to return until she had gone.

The council, after the employment service decided to move its YTS scheme further out of Sheffield and away from the ministrations of the sister, sold on the building. It lay empty for many years, used as a storage area for goods for a while and then finally sold to a property developer in the late 1990s.

The ghost was apparently still in residence when the first tenants moved in and her movements around the building are still heard today. She still appears in the bay window room which is now someone's home. There always seems to be a 'For Sale' sign on this property so perhaps the ghostly resident has been upsetting people who buy it – who knows? Her heavy footsteps though are still to be heard, we're told, going up and down the metal staircases that are one of the original features in the building.

The Methodist Hall.

But exactly why would she be there in the first place? Well the old Methodist Hall was once used as a cholera hospital when one of the last outbreaks occurred in Sheffield; it was a large space and easily quarantined. The nursing sister may just be following her old profession, caring for those who died and still doing her rounds of the rooms with their sick patients. Even if the others cannot be seen her own presence is still strong.

Britannia Music Hall (West Bar)

The Music Hall was something of a star attraction in its heyday but by the time Mr Phillip Knowles bought it in 1982 it had become dilapidated and was in need of restoration. He restored it and used the premises for The Pink Champagne Wedding Centre. Most of the old trapeze rigging was still there, as were the balconies and seats for over 700 people. The old stage had been used as a loading bay by the previous owners and had suffered quite a lot of damage. The new owner was none-the-less determined to use the premises and bring something of its glamorous past back to life.

The Music Hall ghost first appeared to Mr Knowles next to the toilets on the third floor, as a small, pale vision of a girl in her twenties with auburn ringlets that fell onto her shoulders, and dressed in Edwardian clothes. She kept appearing and often appeared to the staff too. Most of them were not afraid of her and would say 'hello' to her as they went into the stock area where she liked to appear.

One night, while working on a rush order, two workers who were less than happy with her appearances saw the ghost and decided that they'd had enough for the night and left the dress half finished. The ghost had scared both of them enough to make them flee the building. On another occasion Mr Knowles himself fled the building. He was working alone on a dress at night when there was suddenly a great noise from the room upstairs; a sound like thunder. It was as if many feet were drumming on the floors above in applause, in the old way of showing approval for a stage act that had surpassed expectation. Needless to say, Mr Knowles left the building in a hurry and was even reluctant to go into work again the next day.

In 1987 the Wedding Centre closed down and was taken over by Harmony Wedding World which continued in the old Music Hall until its closure in the early 1990s. Door World then took over the premises and this was to be last business to use the building because a huge fire ripped through the building and destroyed most of it in 1992. An effort was made to try and preserve the theatre as it was only one of six of its kind in the country but the money was never found and the building was eventually demolished. The West Bar Motor Company now owns the lots that the old Music Hall sat on. The old building is lost but the ghosts apparently didn't give up as it appears they may have moved onto the next building on our list, The Old Fire Station Museum!

The Old Fire Station Museum (West Bar Green)

This building, constructed in 1897, was a purpose built centre housing the Police Station, Fire Station and Ambulance services for Sheffield. It had a chequered history and was finally given retirement status in 1965. The beautiful building was then left empty until 1968 after which it was occupied by a variety of companies, including Paradise House Ltd, and finally Harrison Office Supplies who used it as a warehouse. After they moved out the building became derelict and was in serious need of repair by the time the South Yorkshire Fire Service Historical Society took it over. In 1984 they began work to turn it into a museum, which now displays items from the service's history covering a period from 1794 to the present day. It opens to schools and parties by appointment in the week but the general public can see the exhibits every Sunday, where you can see the old police cells, the stables that housed the horses that pulled the fire wagons, old equipment and, if you're lucky, the ghost that inhabits the fire station!

The ghost in question isn't the lady from the Music Hall next door but one of the old firemen, still apparently awaiting his call to a fire, dressed in a Victorian uniform. He looks like a sailor and people often ask the volunteer staff why they have a sailor dummy in the exhibit. The uniform is mainly white, with bell bottom trousers, a shirt with a square collar, lanyard and whistle. The

Sheffield Police and Fire Station Museum is a favourite venue for ghost hunters.

ghost wanders around the exhibits and has spoken to people on more than one occasion. When they've found out exactly who (or what?) they've been talking to they've said he was a very polite, quiet man.

But he isn't the only ghost in the building: there are no less than seven others who are reported by psychics and mediums to live in the dormitory at the top of the building, above the museum. Several names have been given by mediums and they tally with records of the time, five of the men have been identified but the two women detected there with them are unknown. Perhaps they were from the Music Hall when it burned down!

Another story from the same premises arises from a charity ghost hunt that took place when a group of friends stayed overnight in the building. One of the group decided she wanted some sleep and found a quiet corner to rest in; a room that had been a police cell in days gone by. She was settling down to rest when she heard footsteps outside the cell, footsteps that came from outside the building where there used to be an old parade ground and prisoner exercise yard. She could hear the gravel moving under the feet for about an hour. Her friend who came to wake her found her wide awake and staring at the back wall of the cell she was in. They couldn't remember exactly what was behind this wall and couldn't take a look as the windows were blacked out. When the sun rose they went out to look and found that a small building had been added on over the courtyard (it was built in the late 1940s) to house equipment.

Fire Station, Sheffield.

Sheffield police and fire station when it was in use.

Prisoners by this time, apparently, were not held at the station at all and so the courtyard was used for other things. She put her experience down to a ghostly echo from the time prisoners were given air and exercise in this courtyard outside the cell wall.

An investigation set up by the Sheffield Paranormal Society in 2006 found several anomalies in the building (temperature, sound, scents and noises), but one that caught my attention was given to me by the photographer who furnished most of the modern photographs in this book. He told me of his experience on the ghost hunt: 'I was sitting alone in the top of the building where the old firemen's beds were, on a vigil just waiting for anything unusual to happen. There were no sounds or movements out of the ordinary when suddenly there was a sharp smell of sulphur that hung around for at least a minute, like an old match had been struck to light a pipe or cigarette. The scent was out of place as the entire building is a smoke-free zone and none of the other ghost hunters smoked.' He's not the only person to have reported the scent of sulphur in the building, as if someone had just lit a match and waved it out quickly: several other visitors have smelled the same thing over the years. Whether it's an old fireman or a policeman having a crafty smoke we'll never know, but the evidence is around if your nose is keen enough to catch it.

The Old Don Picture House (West Bar)

The cinema opened in 1912 with capacity for 950 people and a large orchestra. It ran as a picture house and cinema until 1958, just after it acquired a new bigger screen and sound equipment in 1957. The ghost that haunts here is Mr Potter the projectionist, who is known for wearing plus fours, a tweed jacket and a brown overall covering everything.

The building itself has gone through many changes over the years, from a cinema, to a carpet warehouse, to a furniture store and a discount superstore and now a storage facility. At the top of the building there are two swing doors that open and close of their own accord. Workmen refurbishing the building saw the doors open and swing shut as if someone had come through them. One workman even saw Mr Potter enter the toilets just before him and looking around the small space was quite perturbed to find that he was alone in the room as well as the entire building.

Mr Potter devoted his life to the cinema. He never missed a performance and even cycled to work during the Blitz, putting the customers before his own safety. Jeffrey Beardow, who was the junior projectionist, once went back on a visit after the cinema had closed and heard the familiar rumble of the projectors under his feet and asked the staff if they'd kept the projectors running. The staff looked blankly at him and wondered what he was talking about. Jeffrey took the staff to the room that used to be the projection booth. Light and noise were coming from under the door and when he swung the door wide there was nothing but a burnt out room – there had been a fire in the room recently and the floorboards were unsafe. But both Jeffrey and the staff had heard sounds and seen light from under the doorway.

The last manager of the Armadillo Safe Store which currently occupies the building had a nasty surprise from Mr Potter. He likes to creep up behind people and call out their names making them jump; he used to do this to his junior Jeffrey Beardow in the cinema days. The storage house is now filled with CCTV cameras everywhere filming everything that goes on in the building; we can only wonder if Mr Potter has become a star in his own movies instead of showing them. He's still whispering in people's ears as we've had tales of him doing this to customers at the building, but exactly how he finds out their names we have no idea.

The River Don

The River Don has many tales to tell but one that never ceases to shock and amaze is the one of the flood that claimed so many lives. The disaster has been termed 'The Forgotten Disaster of Sheffield' and has passed into history forgotten by the rest of the country. The Don was fierce and terrible the night the Dale Dyke Dam broke, 12 March 1864. The small rivers that filled the dam were let free to flood into the wide and uncontrolled Don. A tidal wave swept all before it, killing over 800 people in its course down the valley. Many were killed in collisions with the pieces of machinery that were pulled along in the turbulent waters and the ghosts that occur because of it are strung all along the course of the flood.

One such set of ghosts resided in a small workshop area still used today as office spaces, the courtyard in the middle open to the skies at Kelham Island. There's a crack that can be seen

The Old Don Picture House, now a storage facility, still has a 'working projectionist'!

from the road in the middle wall of the courtyard and this is where the flood hit and made the entire building shift. After the floodwaters had receded a little the bodies that were washed up here were left in the open courtyard to be identified. The bodies were not alone as the souls of the dead were still there with them and it's these people that are still felt in the courtyard to this day. A gentleman who used to work there felt the touch of the dead when he had to cross the courtyard: it disturbed him so much that he began to walk around the edge as his other colleagues did. No one ever walked directly across the courtyard without shuddering and many visitors asked why the staff walked around the edge.

More ghosts can be found in the Ship Inn at Shalesmoor. The two ghosts in question are of two sailors who were leading a boat up the small tunnel into the public house. It was a spot where untaxed and therefore illegal alcohol was brought into the pub to be sold. The men were drowned in the tunnel as the surge went past, filling the small space and crushing their bodies against the full barrels. Their bodies weren't recovered but ever since then they've been seen and felt in the public house on many occasions – their presence is one of a quiet, shared existence with landlord and landlady. They're often sighted wearing their distinctive striped shirts drinking a pint at the bar or seated alone in the back rooms.

Another, sadder, tale is that of the 'White Children' who seem to haunt the area around Corporation Street. These small figures have been seen by several drivers who have slammed on brakes to avoid the children running across the road only to find no sign of them when they've stopped. I myself have seen these small ghosts whilst walking home along Corporation Street late at night with my wife; they were between the ages of six and ten. Dressed in white or grey smocks they were playing something like hide and seek between the buildings. We stopped to see if we could get a better look at them but they'd disappeared in the middle of a roadway. The flood killed many children, the bodies of whom were never found to be given a Christian burial or last rites. The debris and mud covered a vast area and many bodies were torn apart in the churning water. These children still play in the streets where their small bodies lay, now under tarmac and buildings built over their unknown graves. Although in recent times the area has seen massive redevelopment, with new buildings and apartments going up and disturbing the ground, we expect their shades to be seen on a more regular basis.

There is a rhyme about the Don (or the Dun as it was once called) and its reputation for claiming lives, which goes 'The sliming shelving River Dun, Every year a daughter or a son'. One set of incidents has caused some speculation about the tales of the River Don and her predilection for young strong men to embrace in her watery arms. They all occurred within a space of three years; the first occurred at a place called Hexthorpe (which means in Anglo Saxon, 'Place of the Witch') just inside Doncaster. A young boy was swimming in the river just past a local beauty spot with his friends when he suddenly disappeared from view, he came up spluttering and reaching out for help. But before anyone could get to him he went under again. The other children, instead of helping him, stood frozen to the bank as he drowned. His hands could be seen out of the water asking for rescue but his face never cleared the surface. When the police came to take statements from the children they all said the same thing, that someone had held him under the surface and a dark shape had been seen in the middle of the river which had moved away once the boy had been killed. His body had then surfaced and floated downstream to be picked up near Conisborough. When the body was examined the boy's ankles were found to be marked with ridges as if he'd been held tight by gnarled hands, the river was dragged to see if there was anything that could have caused the marks but nothing was found.

Another incident occurred by The Boat Inn at Sprotborough (upstream from Hexthorpe). This time it was a healthy nineteen year-old man who drowned. He supposedly fell into the river head first. His friends were quite sure that he'd been perfectly happy with his new car, new job and girlfriend and had been looking forward to going on holiday the week after his death. He was also a medal-winning swimmer but he was found twelve feet below the bank floating face down in deep water. When the body was pulled from the water the regulars just shook their heads and kept their backs to the river as if they knew it was something that could happen here. At the post mortem the body was examined for traces of foul play but none were found except that he had marks on his ankles as if he'd been grabbed from behind by someone lower than him and already in the water. When the police went back to look at the place where the man had been standing, a little way away, were strange marks on the bank as if someone or something had brushed against the mud before falling back into the water. The case was registered as an accidental death but the last story in this series concerning deaths along the river was a little more mysterious.

A man was walking down the tow path in Rotherham on his way home from a party in the town centre where he'd been celebrating Christmas with his friends. He'd been especially lucky having just found work after a few years of being unemployed, and his girlfriend was expecting

Ladies Bridge over the Don. Here debris from the flood became stuck under the stone arches, bodies stacked alongside broken homes and machinery.

their first child which he was awaiting with eager anticipation. Everything about his life was good and he had a great future ahead of him. He left the party quite sober because he had to drive his pregnant girlfriend to her mother's the next day and wanted to be safe. He never reached home, his car was caught on CCTV camera going down the tow path, one camera stops filming him and another would have caught him in a few seconds but he never reappeared on the other camera. He was reported missing and family and friends were very concerned for him. He was found in the Don at Mexborough in the following March, lodged under a tree. His clothes were the same as the ones he'd been wearing at Christmas the year before and his body had managed to get through two locks without being seen. The place he turned up at had been at one point a marsh where other bodies had been found in the past. The body was in too poor a state to see if there were any marks on it like the other two.

Many years ago the blood from the slaughter houses of both Sheffield and Doncaster was drained directly into the waters; men would say it made the river 'calmer' if they did this. In point of fact the docks at Doncaster had no accidental drownings recorded there at all until the practice stopped and blood was collected instead to be made into animal feed.

Even though the River Don has a dark reputation she also has a giving side to her. It's said that if you stand on Ladies Bridge and hold a piece of silver in your left hand and make a sincere wish (for something you 'need' not what you 'want') she'll give you what you require within seven days when you throw the silver in the river.

The Washington Pub (Fitzwilliam Street)

The public house that sits to the side of Devonshire Green has been there for many years though the steelworks it once serviced have long gone, destroyed in the Blitz of 1940. The inn somehow survived the war. Maybe it was fate but others tend to think that the building was being looked after by the older residents. The pub has been used constantly since its opening and its ghost tends to make its presence felt when things are being changed. When the pub had its refit upstairs a ghost was heard walking about on the wooden floor above the main bar in the afternoons. There was one problem though – as the floor had been removed to do rewiring for the main bar below. The footsteps that were heard couldn't have come from the actual floor as it was all stacked in the long corridor above.

The ghost also used to come down into the bar on quiet days and move things around for the staff to find, hiding objects and sometimes even shifting the keys for the front door. The ghost is quite quiet these days but it still makes an occasional appearance when the pub is quiet and open. The modern changes that have been undertaken aren't entirely to his or her taste but they still love the building enough to stay there. Which leads us to another ghost who moved buildings when his own was demolished to make way for a new development of shops and bars.

West One Development (Devonshire Green)

Now this new development has only been built for around three years but the ghost that haunts it used to live in the old pub that was on the same space as the new buildings. This ghost is an old gentleman who used to walk into the pub, nod to the bar staff and then continue walking through a wall into the gent's toilets. He would then reappear a few minutes later and sit in one of the old cubicles with a pint of beer. He'd be there until the pub began to fill and then he'd suddenly disappear only to reappear just before closing time to walk out of the pub the same way he came in.

When the pub was demolished the ghost went away for a while but he reappeared in the first year of the building being used. A couple had been living in their new apartment in this new, large block for around three months when things began to go missing; keys, money, a single earring, buttons, all vanished to reappear again in odd places. One set of keys was found in a plant pot outside the front door. The keys weren't for the apartment: they were work keys, kept in a bag which was zipped up for security.

The Washington pub in Fitzwilliam Street where a ghost's footsteps were heard on floorboards that were no longer there.

Yet this wasn't the only trick the ghost had up its sleeve. The man once took his washing down to the washroom where the machines were kept. While trying to open the door with one hand, balancing the full basket with the other, he noticed an old man reading a newspaper, sitting on top of one of the dryers. He remembered thinking 'You could at least have helped me with the door'. As he dropped the entire basket load on the floor the old man did not move or look at him. There was only one door into and out of the washroom and when he finally opened the door and got inside he found that there was no one else in the room. The old man had disappeared. He asked several other residents who used the room if they too had seen the old man and they had, thinking it was a resident's father or friend. When he told me this story I mentioned the one about the ghostly resident of the pub that had once stood on this site but was demolished. When I described him the young man paled and said that it described the old man to a 'T'.

Sheffield ghosts tend to have this habit of moving into places that used to house their old homes and we're always on the lookout for more first hand accounts and tales of ghostly experiences. If you have any tales yourself please don't hesitate to tell us, we're always pleased to hear about the experiences people have had. Many ghosts have been seen and reported on over the years and are still active in Sheffield today. Please come and take the tour yourself and see me, Mr Dreadful, and get the full story about the ghosts of our city. There's always more to discover, just down the road, than you think!

Park Hill Flats

These large modern buildings were designed by Jack Lynn and Ivor Smith in the 1950s and construction was finished in 1961. The building itself was given Grade II listed status in 1998, a 'Streets in the Sky' idea that aimed to provide community living in comfort and harmony. Unfortunately not everything worked out well for the communities that moved into the new blocks although in many ways they provided better accommodation than the slums they replaced.

Having so many people living cheek by jowl and under the economic stresses that were ravaging Sheffield it's no surprise that the building had all kinds of visitors, some who've never left and we're going to hear about one in particular.

One family has a resident spirit that has been with them ever since they moved into their home. They didn't find it much of a nuisance at first, although things would go missing occasionally, but being a young family it wasn't too unusual for things to be misplaced only to be found later. It was when the two girls of this family began to grow up and reached puberty the spirit decided to let itself be known to them. The girls were twins and they shared a room but they noticed that one corner of one room would never get warm. Both girls began to have dreams of someone being in their room, someone who stood in the corner watching them.

The presence never seemed to do anything but watch but then one of the sisters moved into another room in the flat and the spirit seemed to move with her. It seemed to become more active and would sit on the bed, making a cold spot in the bed next to her and a depression in the mattress. Needless to say when she became aware of this she moved out of the bed and went to sleep in the front room of the flat. Despite these visitations the family have continued to live in the flat and try to cope as best they can.

The flats are about to go under extensive renovation. Urban Splash has great plans for the structure which include giving it back some of the pride and joy it once had by refurbishing the flats that are salvageable. They know of this ghost and its habits but as yet we gather they've not asked it to leave or to seek help in removing this visitor. Let's hope the new building work doesn't disturb it and cause any further trouble.

There is another story linked to this imposing building – a small black dog has been seen running along the wide public walkways. It was once a beloved pet owned by someone who lived on the ground floor of this large apartment block. A mixture of terrier and labrador, the dog used to run around greeting people it met and basically having fun when it was allowed out of the flat. The dog was rehoused when the owner died of old age and taken to another part of the city to live out its own old age. The old dog has apparently been dead now for a number of years yet is repeatedly seen by residents who lived on Long Henry Row. One young family got used to greeting the dog every time they saw it but were then told by their next door neighbour that the dog was a ghost. It appears that the dog only began to appear in the flats again where it had lived happily with its old owner after it had died at its new home.

Carbrook Hall

Carbrook Hall is often described as the most haunted public house in Sheffield it does have it's ghost of that we're not contesting but as to its being the most haunted, we're not so sure. That its the most regularly seen and experienced ghost we cannot doubt, as there is a long history of haunting experiences claimed by the regulars who use the pub today. This story describes an incident told to us by a gentleman who went to the pub specifically to see if he could get to see the famous ghost.

The original Carbrook Hall was built in 1462 but then replaced by the current hall in 1583, built by Sir John Bright (the same John Bright who drove out the Royalists from the castle). It is Sir John that is the main ghost of the building. Our intrepid young explorer had gone to the pub with his girlfriend to see if the stories were true. Taking a seat in the main bar he spent a quiet evening without seeing or hearing anything untoward happening and was beginning to feel quite let down by the ghost. At least that was until the ghost suddenly tried to tip a full table of beer glasses over him. He was sitting talking quietly to his girlfriend when the table suddenly pitched forward as if someone had smashed into the table almost spilling the table's contents all over him. No one else was even near the table. Impressed by this demonstration they both left determined to come back and with more people next time. On their second visit they were disappointed but intend to try again. Perhaps Sir John wasn't in the mood to entertain on this occasion. Suffice it to say that he has been seen and felt regularly by many of the regulars before and since but like many ghosts he prefers to perform when he wants to and not just because someone is watching for him.

Tram Ghost

The ghost of an elderly man has been seen numerous times on the Middlewood tram. He apparently catches the tram at the Middlewood tram stop, rides it toward town but fades out and disappears just as he gets to Hillsborough. Who is this strange passenger and why does he make this journey? In the first two years of the tram service an elderly gentleman regularly got on at the tram at Middlewood terminus and took the ride into the city. Unfortunately one day he had a heart attack and died in his seat. It was only when he was on the return journey to Middlewood that the conductor noticed him and that he had not moved. Finding the old gentleman dead he called for help and he was taken from the tram.

Ever since he died, it seems, he has continued to ride the tram, perhaps trying to complete his unfinished journey. He rides from the Middlewood tram stop to the city centre where he just fades away. Conductors have walked toward him to take his fare only to see him blink out in front of them. Drivers have sometimes seen him getting on the tram, even opening the doors and then taking his seat but when they look for him later, he's nowhere to be seen. He is white haired and thinly built, and dressed in a grey coat and flat cap.

Ponds Forge tram stop with the Park Hill flats looming in the background.

John Watts Building – West Bar

This building was once the workshop of Watts the cutlery and razor makers and has seen some accidents and death over its history. It's the modern conversion of this building we're concerned with here. The entire building and surrounds were the casting, finishing and polishing works and in its heyday the complex was in use night and day.

The building has been derelict for many years now. It backs onto the West Bar Police Station and was looked onto by the police officers who were having a break or a quiet cigarette behind their own building. There is a ghost story connected with this building about an accountant who was stealing money from the business in the Second World War. When he thought he was about to be caught he committed suicide in his office, a window that looks back onto the Police station. More than once they went over to check the empty building after hearing what sounded like the echo of a gunshot. The flash of what could have been a shot was sometimes also seen by men coming out of the station, lighting up the window where the accountant reputedly blew his brains out with a gun.

Perhaps it's this man's ghost that made itself known to the demolition team that was gutting the buildings later to convert them for housing. Some workmen standing next to the demolition machinery they'd been using to rip up old concrete and brick from the old grind house were shocked when a piece of concrete about ten feet square threw itself towards them. The men were horrified to see another piece began to shudder and look as if it too was coming their way. The men left the site with some speed and had to be persuaded back to finish the demolition work before the builders could come in and reconstruct the interior.

Many believe that a ghost is the residual energy of a person, left behind when the physical body dies. Following a violent death much more energy is created than following a natural death. This building had been used as a workshop but it was also a temporary hospital during the Sheffield cholera outbreak that once ravaged the area. When the accountant's death added its energy to the building by committing suicide he was perhaps just adding to the already large store of it that was resting in the bricks and stones from the cholera victims. When the building was destroyed from the inside out the energy had nowhere else to go but discharge itself into poltergeist activity. After this incident things calmed down but the workers were still jumpy about being in the place by themselves. They described the building as constantly 'watching' them, threatening even. Some people appear to be particularly sensitive to energy resting in a building where there has been tragedy and death.

Have you ever experienced something like the tales described in this book? If you have we'd love to hear from you. Please get in touch and we'll listen – we're ready to believe you!

BIBLIOGRAPHY

Pevsner Architectural Guides – Sheffield (Ruth Harman and John Minnis, 2004).
More Sheffield Curiosities – Duncan and Trevor Smith (Hedgerow Publishing, 2000).
Peeks at the Past - Sheffield and its surrounding area – Anne Beedam (Packard Publishing).
The Illustrated Guide to Sheffield – Pawson and Brailsford (1879).
Strange Sheffield – David Clarke and Rob Wilson (2002). *Ghost Hunters Guide to Sheffield* – Valerie Salim (Sheaf Publishing, 2001).

Other local titles published by Tempus

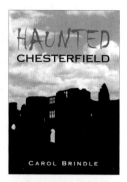

Haunted Chesterfield

CAROL BRINDLE

Take a journey through the darker side of Chesterfield with Blue Badge Guide Carol Brindle who has been leading Ghost Walks in the town for many years. Meet the ghost of George Stephenson at the Pomegranate Theatre, the ghost child of Yorkshire Bank and hear ghostly footsteps in the tower of St Mary and All Saints!

0 7524 4081 0

Sheffield Cinemas

CLIFFORD SHAW AND THE SHEFFIELD CINEMA SOCIETY

The first purpose-built cinema was the Picture Palace in Union Street, which opened in 1910. By the outbreak of war in 1914 there were thirty cinemas and growth accelerated when the 'talkies' arrived. A gradual decline set in during the 1960s as television appeared but we are now witnessing a new surge of interest as the out of town multiplexes provide the venue for watching films. This lavishly illustrated history of Sheffield's cinemas will be a joy to anyone who grew up in the city or who has ever queued outside one on a Saturday night!

0 7524 2293 6

Firth Brown

CATHERINE HAMILTON

The Firth Brown Company was formed in 1930 after the amalgamation of Thomas Firth & Sons and John Brown & Co. Ltd both known throughout the world for their steel products. This book is an illustrated history of one of Sheffield's, and Britain's, greatest steel companies. The splendid collection of old images was selected from the extensive archive held at the Kelham Island Museum.

0 7524 1741 X

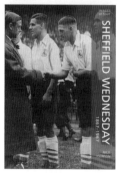

Sheffield Wednesday 1867-1967

NICK JOHNSON

This selection of old photographs charts the first 100 years of a proud, well-supported club from the city that gave organised football to the world. From its birth as an offshoot of a cricket club, through to Football League and FA triumphs the book features insights into everyday life of the players and the club.

0 7524 2720 2

If you are interested in purchasing other books published by Tempus, or in case you have difficulty finding any Tempus books in your local bookshop, you can also place orders directly through our website

www.tempus-publishing.com